INTERCESSORY
PRAYER
ISN'T
Pretty!

DR. BARBARA A. PALMER

Intercessory Prayer Isn't Pretty!

Published by
Kingdom Publishing, LLC
1350 Blair Drive, Odenton, MD 21113

First printed in the U.S.A.

Scripture quotations marked (KJV) are taken from the KING JAMES VERSION, public domain.

ISBN: 978-1-967006-17-5 (Paperback)
ISBN: 978-1-967006-18-2 (Ebook)

Book cover design by Antonio M. Palmer
Book cover painting by Antonio M. Palmer

DEDICATION

I dedicate this book to my first spiritual father, Overseer Julius Crawford, who taught me the value of prayer, seeking God's face, yielding and surrendering to His voice.

ACKNOWLEDGEMENTS

I acknowledge every intercessor who has said yes to God in the secret place.

Those who have prayed through weariness, grief, misunderstanding, and spiritual resistance—yet refused to release the assignment.

I honor the intercessors who cover leaders, families, churches, communities, and nations—often unseen, often unthanked, but always heard by heaven.

To the prayer partners, armor bearers, midnight intercessors, and gatekeepers—your prayers have sustained me, protected vision, shifted atmospheres, and carried others when they could not carry themselves.

Above all, I give glory to God, who calls, equips, and empowers intercessors to partner with Him in the earth. May this book strengthen your resolve, affirm your calling, and remind you that your prayers matter—more than you will ever know.

TABLE OF CONTENTS

Part II: Training the Intercessor

Part III: Responsibility and Endurance

FOREWORD

Why This Book Matters Now

Intercession has never been optional for the people of God. From the earliest pages of Scripture to the formation of the early church, those who stood between heaven and earth were entrusted with more than prayer—they were entrusted with responsibility. They did not merely speak to God; they listened for Him. They did not simply react to crisis; they intercepted it. They did not pray to be seen; they prayed to preserve life, purpose, and covenant.

Yet in our time, intercession has often been misunderstood.

It has been reduced to emotional expression rather than spiritual execution, volume rather than vigilance, and intensity rather than intelligence. In many settings, intercessors have been encouraged to feel deeply but not trained to discern clearly. The result has been prayer gatherings filled with passion but lacking precision, sincerity without strategy, and zeal without sustained fruit.

This book confronts that reality with clarity and courage.

Intercessory Prayer Is Not Pretty does not romanticize prayer. It does not flatter the intercessor. It does not offer shortcuts or sensationalism. Instead, it calls intercessors back to biblical sobriety, spiritual discipline, and covenantal responsibility. It names what many have felt but could not articulate: that true intercession is often quiet, weighty, unseen, and misunderstood—but profoundly effective.

This is not a book about how to pray longer.

It is a book about how to pray accurately.

What sets this work apart is its insistence that intercession must be governed by discernment rather than emotion. Dr. Barbara Palmer writes not as a theorist, but as a practitioner—one who has carried weight, endured seasons of obscurity, and learned through obedience how heaven actually entrusts intercessors with responsibility. The language of the situation room, assignment, posture, and *DEFCON* levels is not creative metaphor—it is spiritual reality explained with clarity.

This book does what few intercessory works dare to do: it trains the reader to pause, listen, and respond rather than rush, react, or perform.

You will not find hype here.

You will find instruction.

You will find correction.

You will find alignment.

And if you are willing, you will find yourself being re-formed.

This book is especially timely. We live in an age of constant noise, instant reaction, and emotional volatility—both in the world and, too often, in the church. God is once again raising up watchmen who can see clearly, speak sparingly, and stand faithfully. He is looking for intercessors who understand timing, who can distinguish peace from passivity, urgency from panic, and revelation from assumption.

This book equips such people.

If you are looking for prayer that makes you feel powerful, this book may unsettle you.

If you are looking for prayer that positions you responsibly, it will transform you.

Read slowly.

Pray honestly.

Receive correction humbly.

And understand this as you begin: if God has drawn you to this book, it is not because you are weak—but because you are being trained.

Intercession is not pretty.

But it is trusted work.

PREFACE

Why This Manual Exists

Intercessory prayer has always been costly. From Genesis to Revelation, those who stood between heaven and earth were never casual participants in spiritual life. They were watchers, gatekeepers, burden-bearers, and defenders. They carried weight long before they carried words. They discerned danger before it manifested. They stood in gaps others did not see and absorbed pressure others could not explain.

Yet somewhere along the way, intercession in many modern contexts has been reduced to emotional expression rather than spiritual execution.

This book exists because God interrupted that pattern.

Several years ago, the Lord spoke to me clearly and unmistakably: "Dismantle what you have called intercession, and rebuild it according to My design." What had once been a disciplined, strategic prayer culture had slowly devolved into something else—well-intentioned, sincere, passionate, but ineffective. Intercessors were praying from their emotions instead of from revelation. They were leaving prayer gatherings exhausted rather than empowered, burdened rather than covered, vocal rather than victorious.

The tears were real.

The passion was genuine.

But the fruit was inconsistent.

The Lord showed me that much of what we had labeled "deep intercession" was actually emotional discharge. Intercessors were releasing pressure instead of applying authority. Prayer gatherings had become places of spiritual venting rather than centers of heavenly intelligence. And while the presence of God was often felt, the strategies of God were rarely received.

This manual was born out of that correction.

The Difference Between Presence and Assignment

One of the most dangerous misunderstandings in prayer culture is the assumption that feeling God automatically means fulfilling God's assignment. Scripture never equates spiritual sensation with spiritual success. In fact, many of the most effective intercessory moments in Scripture were marked not by emotional display but by disciplined obedience, watchfulness, and silence before action.

Moses did not feel powerful standing before Pharaoh—but heaven backed him. Esther did not feel safe approaching the king—but history shifted because she did. Daniel did not feel triumphant in exile—but his disciplined prayer life altered empires. Jesus did not feel relieved in Gethsemane—but His submission there secured redemption for the world.

Intercession is not validated by how intense it feels but by how accurately it aligns with heaven.

This book draws a firm line between the presence of God and the purpose of God in prayer. Worship ushers us into His presence—but intercession requires that we stay long enough to receive instruction. The Holy Spirit does not merely want to comfort intercessors; He wants to train them.

Why Emotion Alone Is Not Enough

Emotion is not the enemy. God created emotion, and Scripture affirms it. Tears, travail, groaning, worship, tongues, and expressive prayer all have biblical precedent. The problem arises when emotion becomes the operating system instead of a response to revelation.

An intercessor who prays only from emotion will pray loudly but inaccurately.

An intercessor who prays from revelation will pray precisely—even quietly—and still move heaven.

The enemy does not fear emotional intercessors. He fears trained ones.

Satan has no issue with prayer gatherings that stay in worship indefinitely, never shift posture, never receive instruction, never identify targets, and never enforce authority. Emotional exhaustion keeps intercessors distracted, discouraged, and dependent on the next "release" rather than grounded in assignment.

This manual exists to confront that system.

The Situation Room of Heaven

The language of the Situation Room is not metaphorical—it is instructional. In the natural world, a situation room exists for one purpose: to monitor threats, receive intelligence, assess risk, and determine response. No one enters casually. No one speaks unnecessarily. No one operates emotionally. Every movement is measured because lives are at stake.

The Lord revealed to me that intercessors are meant to function in the same way spiritually.

Intercession is heaven's situation room on earth.

God reveals information to intercessors not so they can discuss it, broadcast it, or dramatize it—but so they can pray it through. Spiritual intelligence is not given for exposure; it is given for interception. When God trusts an intercessor with insight, it is because He expects precision, confidentiality, and obedience.

This book trains intercessors to recognize when they are being invited into that room—and how to behave once inside.

From Outer Courts to the Holy of Holies

Much of modern prayer culture remains stuck in the outer courts. There is sound, movement, expression, and activity—but very little silence, posture, or listening. The Holy of Holies, however, is not accessed through noise but through surrender. It is a place of bowing, waiting, and receiving instruction before action.

Scripture teaches that boldness does not mean recklessness. Access does not mean familiarity. Authority does not mean chaos. Intercessors who do not learn how to shift realms will never sustain long-term effectiveness.

This manual intentionally trains intercessors to:

- Recognize spiritual gates
- Shift postures appropriately
- Discern timing and threat levels
- Pray from instruction, not impulse
- Understand when worship is preparation and when warfare is required

Why Assignments Matter

One of the primary reasons intercessors burn out is not because they pray too much—but because they pray without assignment. Carrying everything is not spiritual maturity; it is spiritual misalignment. God has never asked one intercessor to cover everything. He assigns territories, people, seasons, and functions.

Assignment preserves stamina.

Assignment sharpens authority.

Assignment clarifies responsibility.

This book dismantles the false belief that effective intercessors must feel everything deeply. Instead, it teaches intercessors how to steward what God has actually given them to carry—and how to release what He has not.

DEFCON Intercession: Responding, Not Reacting

One of the most revelatory frameworks in this book is the concept of DEFCON Intercession Levels. Heaven does not respond to every threat the same way—and neither should intercessors. Not every prayer moment is an emergency. Not every burden requires travail. Not every situation calls for warfare.

Discernment is the difference between reacting and responding.

This manual equips intercessors to recognize levels of spiritual threat and to adjust posture, language, authority, and endurance accordingly. Intercessors who cannot discern levels will overreact to minor issues and underreact to critical ones.

Heaven trusts those who know how to read the moment.

Who This Book Is For

This book is not for the spiritually curious.

It is not for those seeking emotional experiences.

It is not for those who want prayer without responsibility.

This book is for:

- Intercessors who feel the weight but lack language
- Prayer leaders who want structure without quenching the Spirit
- Churches ready to move from emotional prayer culture to strategic intercession
- Watchmen who know something is shifting but need training to respond
- Believers God has trusted with insight, urgency, and burden

If you have ever left a prayer gathering feeling drained instead of directed, this book is for you. If you have sensed danger before evidence appeared, this book is for you. If you know God is calling you higher but have not known how to shift, this book is for you.

How to Use This Manual

This book is designed to be read slowly and practiced intentionally. It is not meant to be rushed. Each chapter builds upon the last. Skipping posture will compromise authority. Ignoring assignment will weaken endurance.

I recommend:

- Reading each chapter prayerfully
- Pausing at activations and actually completing them
- Journaling revelations and assignments
- Revisiting chapters during different seasons
- Using this book to train prayer teams, not just individuals

This is not inspirational reading. It is spiritual training.

A Final Word Before You Begin

Intercession is not pretty.

It is not glamorous.

It is not always rewarding in the moment.

It often requires silence instead of sound, endurance instead of excitement, and obedience instead of emotion.

But it is trusted work.

If you are reading this book, it is because God has already trusted you with weight. This manual does not give you authority—it teaches you how to operate in the authority you already carry.

Read carefully. Pray accurately. Stand faithfully.

Heaven is watching.

Footnotes

1. E. M. Bounds, *Power Through Prayer* (Grand Rapids: Baker Books, 1991), 11–15.
2. Andrew Murray, *With Christ in the School of Prayer* (New Kensington, PA: Whitaker House, 1981), 23–27.
3. Dutch Sheets, *Intercessory Prayer* (Ventura, CA: Regal Books, 1996), 41–58.
4. Derek Prince, *Shaping History Through Prayer and Fasting* (Old Tappan, NJ: Chosen Books, 1997), 89–102.
5. Watchman Nee, *The Authority of the Believer* (New York: Christian Fellowship Publishers, 1972), 45–63.
6. Gordon D. Fee, *God's Empowering Presence: The Holy Spirit in the Letters of Paul* (Peabody, MA: Hendrickson, 1994), 877–890.

INTRODUCTION

Intercessory Prayer Is Not Pretty

Intercessory prayer has never been a gentle assignment. Scripture does not present it as tidy, predictable, or emotionally comfortable. True intercession is weighty, disruptive, and often misunderstood—even by those called to it. It requires discernment beyond feeling, endurance beyond enthusiasm, and obedience beyond preference. Intercession is not the art of sounding spiritual; it is the responsibility of standing between heaven and earth until heaven's will prevails.

Yet in many modern prayer cultures, intercession has been softened, diluted, and reduced to emotional expression. Loudness has been mistaken for authority. Tears have been mistaken for accuracy. Passion has been mistaken for effectiveness. While emotion certainly has a place in prayer, it was never intended to be the governing force of intercession.

This book begins with a necessary correction:

Intercessory prayer is not pretty.

It is not designed to soothe the intercessor.

It is not intended to entertain the room.

It is not measured by how moved we feel afterward.

1

Intercession is measured by what shifts, what is protected, what is dismantled, and what is preserved.

From Emotion to Execution

For years, many intercessors have been trained—implicitly or explicitly—to equate emotional intensity with spiritual depth. If prayer did not involve tears, raised voices, prolonged tongues, or visible travail, it was often assumed to be shallow or ineffective. Over time, this created a culture where expression replaced execution and release replaced responsibility.

But intercession is not therapy.

Prayer can involve emotional release, but intercession demands strategic response. An intercessor may feel deeply, but must never be led by feeling. The Holy Spirit does not merely stir emotion; He reveals intelligence. He does not only comfort; He commissions.

When intercessors pray without direction, they often leave exhausted but unchanged. When they pray without assignment, they carry burdens they were never authorized to hold. When they pray without strategy, they produce sound without impact.

Scripture never presents intercession as random. Biblical intercessors prayed with awareness, specificity, and alignment to God's will. They did not guess. They listened. They did not react. They responded.

This introduction exists to reset expectations.

The Question That Changes Everything

There is a question every intercessor must learn to ask before opening their mouth:

What is the assignment right now?

Not every prayer moment is the same. Not every burden carries the same urgency. Not every situation requires the same posture. Failure to discern the moment results in misplaced energy and diminished authority.

Too often, prayer gatherings move quickly into emotional expression without pausing long enough to identify:

- What is under threat?
- What needs protection?
- What is forming unseen?
- What realm is being engaged?
- What response is heaven requiring?

Intercession that does not begin with discernment will always default to emotion. And emotion, when ungoverned by revelation, becomes noise.

The Outer Courts Problem

Many believers have learned how to enter God's presence but have never been trained to remain there long enough to receive instruction. Worship is treated as the destination rather than the doorway. Tears are shed, songs are sung, hands are lifted—but posture never shifts.

Scripture reveals a clear progression: gates, courts, holy place, Holy of Holies. Each realm requires a different posture. Each level carries increased responsibility. Access increases accountability.

The outer courts are filled with sound.

The Holy of Holies is marked by reverence and listening.

Intercessors who remain in the outer courts will experience God emotionally but never engage Him strategically. The Holy of Holies is where intercessors bow before they speak, listen before they act, and receive instruction before releasing words.

God is not calling intercessors to louder prayer—He is calling them to deeper posture.

Why the Enemy Fears Strategic Intercession

The enemy does not fear prayer gatherings that never shift posture. He does not fear emotional outbursts that lack authority. He does not fear intercessors who exhaust themselves without enforcing heaven's will.

But he deeply fears intercessors who know how to:

- Discern timing
- Recognize gates
- Identify targets
- Shift levels
- Pray from instruction
- Sustain endurance

Strategic intercession disrupts plans before they manifest. It intercepts assignments while they are still forming. It dismantles weapons before they are deployed. Emotional prayer reacts after damage occurs. Strategic intercession prevents damage altogether.

This is why the enemy works so diligently to keep intercessors tired, unfocused, offended, overburdened, and emotionally driven. An intercessor governed by emotion will pray often—but rarely effectively.

Intercession as Responsibility, Not Performance

One of the most subtle dangers in prayer culture is performance. When prayer becomes performative, it shifts from obedience to display. Volume increases, posture decreases, and discernment fades. Intercessors begin praying to be heard rather than praying to enforce.

Jesus directly addressed this issue when He warned against prayer that seeks attention rather than alignment with God's will. True intercession is rarely impressive to observers—but it is devastating to the enemy.

Intercession requires restraint.

It requires silence.

It requires listening.

It requires submission.

Heaven does not respond to how loud we pray—it responds to how aligned we are.

The Burden Without Language

Many intercessors carry weight they cannot explain. They sense urgency without clarity. They feel heaviness without instruction. They experience pressure without strategy. Over time, this leads to frustration, fatigue, and discouragement.

This book gives language to that burden.

Intercession is not supposed to leave you confused. The Holy Spirit is not the author of ambiguity. When God places weight on an intercessor, He intends to provide understanding, direction, and authority.

This manual trains intercessors to translate burden into action—to move from sensing to strategy.

Why "Not Pretty" Is Necessary Language

The title of this book is intentionally confrontational. It disrupts romanticized ideas of prayer and replaces them with biblical realism. Intercession often involves discomfort, disruption, and endurance. It may require praying when emotions are dry, when results are delayed, and when affirmation is absent.

Pretty prayer seeks atmosphere.

Powerful intercession seeks outcomes.

There will be moments when intercession requires groaning, travail, and tears—but those moments are governed by the Spirit, not emotion. There will also be moments when intercession requires silence, authority, and command.

Intercessors must be trained to discern which is required—and when.

The Call to Maturity

This introduction serves as a call to maturity in prayer. Spiritual infancy relies on feeling. Spiritual maturity relies on obedience. Infants cry when uncomfortable; mature intercessors stand when pressure increases.

The church does not need louder prayers—it needs trained intercessors. Heaven is not looking for dramatic moments; it is looking for disciplined watchmen.

This book does not diminish emotion—it places it in proper order.

Emotion responds to revelation.

Revelation governs action.

Action enforces heaven's will.

What This Book Will Train You to Do

As you continue through this manual, you will be trained to:

- Discern spiritual environments
- Recognize when worship must shift into intercession
- Identify specific prayer targets
- Understand levels of threat and response
- Operate within assignment rather than overwhelm
- Guard spiritual intelligence
- Pray from authority, not anxiety

Each chapter builds toward the central truth that intercessors are not emotional responders—they are strategic agents of heaven.

A Sobering Reality

Intercessory prayer carries accountability. Scripture teaches that to whom much is given, much is required. When God entrusts insight, urgency, or awareness to an intercessor, He expects stewardship.

This book does not exist to excite—it exists to equip.

If you choose to continue reading, you are agreeing to be trained. You are agreeing to grow. You are agreeing to pray differently than before.

You will no longer be able to claim ignorance.

An Invitation, Not an Accusation

This introduction is not written to shame intercessors—it is written to invite them higher. Many have been faithful without training. Many have endured without instruction. Many have stood on walls without support.

God sees that faithfulness.

Now He is calling intercessors into greater clarity.

Intercessory prayer is not pretty—but it is powerful, purposeful, and trusted work.

If you are willing to move beyond emotion into execution, beyond release into responsibility, and beyond sound into strategy, then proceed.

The next chapter begins with the first necessary correction:

Worship is not the target.

Footnotes

1. Andrew Murray, *With Christ in the School of Prayer* (New Kensington, PA: Whitaker House, 1981), 29–35.
2. E. M. Bounds, *Power Through Prayer* (Grand Rapids: Baker Books, 1991), 17–24.
3. Dutch Sheets, *Intercessory Prayer* (Ventura, CA: Regal Books, 1996), 63–79.
4. Derek Prince, *Shaping History Through Prayer and Fasting* (Old Tappan, NJ: Chosen Books, 1997), 41–56.
5. Watchman Nee, *The Authority of the Believer* (New York: Christian Fellowship Publishers, 1972), 71–85.
6. Gordon D. Fee, *God's Empowering Presence* (Peabody, MA: Hendrickson, 1994), 887–894.

PART I
POSTURE BEFORE POWER

CHAPTER 1
WORSHIP IS NOT THE TARGET

Worship is essential. It is holy. It is biblical. It is powerful. But worship—by itself—is not the assignment of the intercessor.

This chapter establishes a foundational correction that must be settled before any intercessor can mature into strategic prayer: worship is the doorway, not the destination. When worship becomes the end goal, intercession never begins. When worship remains the posture, authority is never enforced. When worship is mistaken for the assignment, prayer gatherings feel spiritual but remain unproductive.

Intercessors must learn how to enter through worship and then shift.

The Purpose of Worship in Intercession

Worship serves a specific function in intercessory prayer. It aligns the heart. It stills the soul. It re-centers the mind on who God is rather than what we feel. Worship creates reverence and clears distraction, making the intercessor sensitive to the Holy Spirit's leading.

Scripture affirms this clearly:

"Enter into his gates with thanksgiving, and into his courts with praise: be

thankful unto him, and bless his name." (Psalm 100:4, KJV)

The language of gates and courts is intentional. Worship gives access—but it does not complete the journey. Gates are for entry. Courts are transitional spaces. They are not the throne room.

Intercessors who stop in the courts will experience atmosphere but never strategy. Worship positions us to hear, but intercession requires that we listen long enough to receive instruction.

When Worship Becomes a Hiding Place

One of the most subtle dangers in prayer culture is using worship to avoid responsibility. Worship can become a safe place where no decisions are required, no targets are identified, and no authority is exercised.

Many prayer gatherings linger in worship because it feels good, it feels safe, and it feels familiar. But the Holy Spirit does not only draw us into God's presence—He draws us into God's purpose.

Jesus made this distinction clear:

"The hour cometh, and now is, when the true worshippers shall worship the Father in spirit and in truth." (John 4:23, KJV)

Truth demands alignment. Truth demands response. Truth demands obedience.

Spirit without truth becomes emotional experience. Truth without spirit becomes dry duty. Intercession requires both—but truth governs the moment when worship must shift.

The Error of Endless Worship

Worship that never transitions becomes stagnation. The presence of God is meant to activate, not anesthetize. When worship becomes endless, intercessors remain expressive but ineffective.

Scripture repeatedly shows that worship precedes action:

*   Jehoshaphat worshiped—then received strategy (2 Chronicles 20).
*   Isaiah worshiped—then was commissioned (Isaiah 6).

- The early church worshiped—then fasted, prayed, and sent leaders (Acts 13:1–3).

In each case, worship was the prelude, not the performance.

Intercessors must learn to recognize the moment when the Holy Spirit says, "Shift now."

From Sound to Strategy

Sound alone does not move heaven. Strategy does.

Intercessors often confuse spiritual noise with spiritual authority. Volume increases when clarity is absent. Repetition replaces revelation. Emotion substitutes for instruction.

But intercession is not about how much is said—it is about what is enforced.

Scripture teaches that heaven responds to alignment with God's will:

"If we ask any thing according to his will, he heareth us." (1 John 5:14, KJV)

The will of God is not accessed through emotion—it is accessed through listening.

Why Intercessors Must Pause After Worship

One of the most practical disciplines this book introduces is the discipline of pause.

After worship, intercessors must stop speaking.

Silence is not inactivity; it is attentiveness. The Holy Spirit often releases instruction in moments of stillness. When intercessors rush past silence, they rush past strategy.

"Be still, and know that I am God." (Psalm 46:10, KJV)

Stillness is not passive—it is reverent readiness.

Worship Aligns—Intercession Executes

Worship softens the heart; intercession strengthens the stance.

Worship reminds us who God is; intercession enforces what God wills.

Worship prepares the soil; intercession plants the seed.

If intercessors do not make this shift, prayer gatherings become emotionally fulfilling but spiritually incomplete.

The Danger of Emotional Intercession

Emotion-driven intercession often results in:

- Exhaustion without breakthrough
- Repetition without revelation
- Tears without targets
- Passion without protection

The enemy does not fear emotional prayer. He fears disciplined obedience.

Intercessors must be trained to govern emotion, not suppress it. Emotion responds to revelation—it must never lead it.

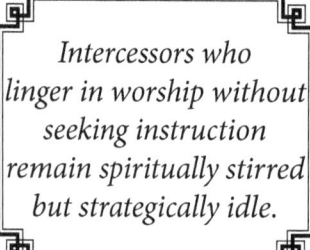

Intercessors who linger in worship without seeking instruction remain spiritually stirred but strategically idle.

Biblical Pattern: Worship → Instruction → Action

Throughout Scripture, God consistently follows this pattern:

1. Encounter – God reveals Himself
2. Instruction – God speaks His will
3. Response – God's servant obeys

Isaiah's encounter illustrates this perfectly:

"I saw also the Lord sitting upon a throne... Then said I, Here am I; send me." (Isaiah 6:1, 8, KJV)

Isaiah did not remain in worship. He was commissioned.

Intercessors who linger in worship without seeking instruction remain spiritually stirred but strategically idle.

Recognizing the Shift

How does an intercessor know when worship must shift?

- The atmosphere settles
- Emotional intensity subsides
- Clarity begins to surface
- Burden sharpens rather than spreads

This is the moment to ask:

"Holy Spirit, what is the assignment right now?"

Failure to ask this question keeps prayer shallow.

When Worship Is the Assignment—and When It Is Not

There are moments when worship is the assignment—especially in seasons of consecration or repentance. But those moments are directed by the Spirit, not assumed by habit.

Intercessors must not default to worship; they must discern.

Discernment distinguishes spiritual maturity from spiritual routine.

A Word to Prayer Leaders

Prayer leaders carry responsibility for facilitating the shift. Leading worship is not the same as leading intercession. Leaders must watch the room, sense the Spirit, and guide posture change.

A leader who refuses to shift keeps the entire room in the outer courts.

Leadership in prayer requires courage—the courage to interrupt comfort for the sake of assignment.

Practical Training: How to Shift from Worship

1. End worship intentionally
2. Call for silence
3. Ask for assignment clarity
4. Wait until instruction surfaces
5. Pray specifically and briefly

Authority does not require length—it requires alignment.

When Worship Is Used to Avoid Warfare

Some intercessors stay in worship because they are uncomfortable with confrontation. Warfare requires authority. Authority requires confidence. Confidence requires knowing who you are in God.

This book will train intercessors to confront resistance—not avoid it.

A Necessary Realignment

Worship is sacred—but it is not the finish line.

Intercessors must learn to move.

> *Some intercessors stay in worship because they are uncomfortable with confrontation.*

Heaven does not need louder worship—it needs obedient execution.

Pray This

Father, thank You for worship that aligns our hearts. Now teach us to shift. Silence our flesh so we can hear Your instruction. Give us courage to move from presence into purpose. Show us the target—and help us hit it.

When This Happens... Pray Like This

When worship lingers without direction:

"Lord, reveal the assignment beneath the atmosphere. Show us what must be protected or confronted right now."

Declarations

- I honor worship, but I do not stop there.
- I move from sound to strategy.
- I pray with clarity and authority.
- I shift when the Spirit leads.

Activation

After your next worship moment, remain silent for five minutes. Write down any instruction, burden, or clarity the Holy Spirit reveals. Pray only what He shows you.

Footnotes

1. Andrew Murray, *With Christ in the School of Prayer* (New Kensington, PA: Whitaker House, 1981), 37–45.
2. E. M. Bounds, *Power Through Prayer* (Grand Rapids: Baker Books, 1991), 29–36.
3. Dutch Sheets, *Intercessory Prayer* (Ventura, CA: Regal Books, 1996), 81–97.
4. Derek Prince, *Shaping History Through Prayer and Fasting* (Old Tappan, NJ: Chosen Books, 1997), 67–74.
5. Watchman Nee, *The Authority of the Believer* (New York: Christian Fellowship Publishers, 1972), 91–104.

CHAPTER 2
WHAT ARE YOU AIMING AT?

Intercessory prayer without a target is spiritual motion without direction. It may be sincere, intense, and time-consuming—but without aim, it produces little impact. This chapter addresses one of the most critical deficiencies in modern prayer culture: the absence of spiritual targeting.

Intercessors are not called to pray randomly. We are called to pray accurately.

> Intercessors are not called to pray randomly. We are called to pray accurately.

The difference between prayer that soothes the intercessor and prayer that shifts outcomes often comes down to one question:

What are you aiming at?

Until this question is answered, intercession remains unfocused. And unfocused prayer, no matter how passionate, rarely produces lasting fruit.

Burden Is Not the Same as Assignment

Many intercessors mistake burden for assignment. They feel weight, heaviness, urgency, or emotional pressure and assume that feeling alone is the instruction to pray. But Scripture teaches that the Holy Spirit does not merely burden—He directs.

A burden without clarity becomes confusion.

A burden without instruction becomes exhaustion.

A burden without aim becomes emotional release.

The Holy Spirit never burdens an intercessor without intending to provide definition. When God places weight on an intercessor, He also intends to reveal where, why, and how to respond.

Too many intercessors pray from sensation instead of revelation. They feel something is wrong but never stop long enough to ask what it is attached to. As a result, they pray broadly when God is calling for precision.

The Watchman's Advantage

Scripture repeatedly identifies intercessors as watchmen. Watchmen do not shout randomly into the night—they observe, discern, and warn with specificity.

"I will stand upon my watch, and set me upon the tower, and will watch to see what he will say unto me." (Habakkuk 2:1, KJV)

Notice the order: stand → watch → see → hear → respond.

A watchman who does not see clearly cannot warn accurately. Likewise, an intercessor who does not identify the target cannot pray effectively.

God does not expect intercessors to guess. He expects them to watch.

Why Random Prayer Weakens Authority

Random prayer feels spiritual, but it lacks enforcement. When intercessors pray without aim, they often:

- Jump from topic to topic
- Pray generally instead of specifically
- Carry multiple burdens without resolution
- Leave prayer unsure of what was actually accomplished

This creates a cycle of fatigue and frustration. Intercessors begin to doubt their effectiveness, not realizing the issue is not devotion—it is direction.

Scripture emphasizes targeted warfare:

"For the weapons of our warfare are not carnal, but mighty through God to the pulling down of strong holds." (2 Corinthians 10:4, KJV)

Strongholds are not pulled down accidentally. They are identified, confronted, and dismantled.

Targeted Prayer Requires Discernment

Discernment is not intuition. It is not suspicion. It is not emotional sensitivity. Discernment is spiritual perception granted by the Holy Spirit.

Discernment answers questions such as:

- Where is the enemy attempting access?
- What is forming beneath the surface?
- Who or what is under threat?
- What timing is involved?
- What level of response is required?

Intercessors who pray without discernment often pray after damage occurs. Intercessors who pray with discernment intercept assignments before manifestation.

From Vague Language to Specific Authority

Vague prayers produce vague results.

Statements such as "Lord, cover everyone," or "God, bless everything," may sound spiritual, but they rarely strike a target. Heaven responds to specificity because specificity reflects obedience.

Jesus modeled targeted prayer. He addressed storms directly. He spoke to sickness by name. He rebuked spirits intentionally. He did not pray broadly when precision was required.

Authority flows through clarity.

The Danger of Over-Carrying

Another reason intercessors avoid targeting is because they feel responsible for everything. When prayer lacks aim, intercessors attempt to cover entire cities, families, churches, and nations in one sitting.

God never intended intercessors to carry everything.

Assignment limits scope so authority can increase. When intercessors attempt to cover what God did not assign, they dilute their effectiveness and strain their stamina.

Targeted prayer protects the intercessor as much as it protects the assignment.

Asking the Right Question Before You Pray

Before releasing words, intercessors must learn to ask:

- "Holy Spirit, what specifically needs prayer right now?"
- "Who is this burden connected to?"
- "Is this a warning, an intercession, or a call to watch?"
- "What scripture aligns with this assignment?"

Prayer that begins with inquiry ends with impact.

The Role of Scripture in Targeted Prayer

Scripture anchors prayer. It prevents emotion from dominating the moment. When intercessors pray without Scripture, emotion often fills the gap.

The Word of God sharpens aim.

Scripture provides:

- Language for authority
- Parameters for alignment
- Confidence in enforcement

Intercessors should never release a prayer they cannot support with the Word.

Why Heaven Responds to Aim

God honors obedience. Targeted prayer demonstrates obedience because it reflects listening. When intercessors pray what God reveals, they partner with heaven rather than performing for it.

"If ye abide in me, and my words abide in you, ye shall ask what ye will, and it shall be done unto you." (John 15:7, KJV)

Abiding produces alignment. Alignment produces authority.

Practical Signs You Have Missed the Target

Intercessors should learn to recognize warning signs that prayer lacked aim:

- You feel drained but unclear afterward
- You cannot articulate what was accomplished
- The same burdens return repeatedly
- There is sound but no shift
- Peace never settles

These are signals—not condemnation—that targeting must improve.

Training the Intercessor to Aim

Targeted intercession is learned, not assumed. It requires discipline, patience, and humility.

Intercessors must be willing to:

- Pause before praying
- Sit in silence without rushing
- Ask clarifying questions
- Release only what God assigns

This discipline feels uncomfortable at first—but it produces precision.

A Word to Group Intercession Settings

Group prayer often struggles with targeting because multiple voices are released simultaneously without agreement. While corporate prayer has power, it must still operate with focus.

Prayer leaders must establish the target before opening the floor.

Agreement amplifies authority. Confusion weakens it.

When the Target Is a Person

When God assigns a person as a target of intercession, confidentiality is essential. The goal is protection, not exposure.

Intercessors must resist the urge to discuss what God reveals. Prayer is the response—not conversation.

> When God assigns a person as a target of intercession, confidentiality is essential. The goal is protection, not exposure.

The Shift From Emotion to Accuracy

This chapter calls intercessors out of vague prayer and into disciplined accuracy. Emotion may initiate awareness—but only discernment completes assignment.

You are not weak because you feel deeply. You become effective when you pray deliberately.

Pray This

Holy Spirit, remove vague prayer from me. Train my eyes to see clearly and my ears to hear accurately. Give me discipline to pause, discern, and aim before I speak. I choose obedience over emotion and accuracy over volume.

When This Happens… Pray Like This

When you feel burdened but unclear:

"Lord, show me exactly what this burden is attached to so I can pray accurately and not exhaust myself unnecessarily."

Declarations

- I do not pray randomly.

- I discern before I speak.
- I aim with spiritual precision.
- I hit the target heaven reveals.

Activation

Set aside ten minutes in prayer. Do not speak until the Holy Spirit identifies one specific target. Write it down. Pray only for that target using Scripture. Stop when peace settles.

Footnotes

1. Dutch Sheets, *Intercessory Prayer* (Ventura, CA: Regal Books, 1996), 99–116.
2. E. M. Bounds, *Power Through Prayer* (Grand Rapids: Baker Books, 1991), 41–48.
3. Andrew Murray, *With Christ in the School of Prayer* (New Kensington, PA: Whitaker House, 1981), 51–59.
4. Derek Prince, *Shaping History Through Prayer and Fasting* (Old Tappan, NJ: Chosen Books, 1997), 83–91.
5. Watchman Nee, *The Authority of the Believer* (New York: Christian Fellowship Publishers, 1972), 109–122.

CHAPTER 3
ENTERING THE HOLY OF HOLIES

Intercessory prayer reaches its highest level of effectiveness when the intercessor understands where they are praying from. Authority in prayer is not only about what is said—it is about position. Many believers pray faithfully yet remain frustrated because they have never been taught how to shift realms spiritually. They pray toward God instead of praying from communion with Him.

This chapter introduces one of the most critical truths every intercessor must understand:

Not every realm of prayer carries the same authority.

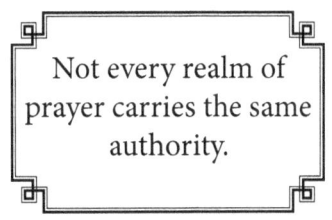

Not every realm of prayer carries the same authority.

There is a difference between praying in the outer courts and praying from the Holy of Holies. One involves access; the other involves proximity. One involves sound; the other involves submission. One involves expression; the other involves responsibility.

God is calling intercessors beyond surface prayer into the place where instruction is released, authority is enforced, and assignments are clarified.

Understanding the Pattern God Established

God has always been intentional about access. From the Tabernacle of Moses to the Temple of Solomon, Scripture reveals a clear spiritual progression: outer court, inner court, Holy Place, Holy of Holies. This pattern was not ceremonial excess—it was divine instruction.

Each realm represented increasing holiness, increasing intimacy, and increasing accountability.

The outer court was public.

The Holy Place was restricted.

The Holy of Holies was exclusive.

Only those authorized could enter—and only with reverence.

This pattern teaches intercessors something essential: greater access requires greater discipline.

Why Many Intercessors Never Move Beyond the Outer Courts

The outer courts are busy. They are loud. They are expressive. They are emotionally engaging. This is where thanksgiving, praise, and worship often flourish. There is movement, sound, and participation.

But the outer courts are not the place of strategy.

> Intercessors who never move beyond the outer courts experience God—but they rarely hear Him clearly.

Many intercessors remain here because it is familiar and affirming. There is little demand for silence, listening, or restraint. Emotion is welcomed and encouraged. But familiarity can become limitation.

Intercessors who never move beyond the outer courts experience God—but they rarely hear Him clearly.

The Holy of Holies: A Place of Posture, Not Performance

The Holy of Holies was not a place of activity. It was a place of presence.

No crowd gathered there. No performance occurred there. No unnecessary movement was permitted there.

It was the place where God spoke.

Scripture declares:

"Let us therefore come boldly unto the throne of grace, that we may obtain mercy, and find grace to help in time of need." (Hebrews 4:16, KJV)

Boldness here does not mean irreverence. It means confidence rooted in submission. The Holy of Holies requires humility, stillness, and attentiveness.

Intercessors who enter this realm understand that prayer begins with listening.

Silence Is Not Absence—It Is Preparation

One of the greatest challenges for intercessors entering the Holy of Holies is silence. Silence feels unproductive to the flesh. But silence is the training ground of discernment.

God often speaks most clearly when the intercessor stops speaking.

"Be still, and know that I am God." (Psalm 46:10, KJV)

Stillness is not inactivity—it is spiritual readiness. Intercessors who cannot tolerate silence will struggle to receive instruction.

The Holy of Holies requires restraint before release.

Hearing Before Speaking

Many intercessors pray at God instead of praying with Him. They enter prayer time already decided on what they will say, what they will address, and how they will pray. This approach leaves no room for divine interruption.

Entering the Holy of Holies requires surrendering the agenda.

God is not impressed by prepared speeches. He is honored by yielded hearts.

"Speak, Lord; for thy servant heareth." (1 Samuel 3:9, KJV)

Intercession begins when the intercessor becomes a servant again.

Why Strategy Is Released in This Realm

The Holy of Holies is where spiritual intelligence is released. This is where God reveals what is forming beneath the surface, what needs protection, and what must be confronted.

God does not release strategy in chaos. He releases it in reverence.

Intercessors who rush through worship and skip stillness often miss instruction entirely. They pray sincerely—but without clarity.

Strategy requires proximity.

The Weight of Responsibility in the Holy of Holies

Access to the Holy of Holies carries weight. God does not reveal sensitive information casually. When He entrusts insight, He expects stewardship.

This is why intercessors must guard what they hear. Revelation is not for discussion—it is for intercession.

Intercessors who gossip revelation forfeit trust.

Why Emotion Must Yield to Discernment

Emotion may accompany intercession, but it must never govern it. The Holy of Holies is not driven by feeling—it is governed by truth.

When intercessors remain emotionally dominant, they often misinterpret what they hear. Emotion distorts perception; discernment clarifies it.

Intercessors must learn to filter emotion through obedience.

Boldness Does Not Eliminate Reverence

Hebrews teaches that we enter boldly—but reverence remains essential. Boldness comes from covenant. Reverence comes from understanding who God is.

The Holy of Holies is not casual access—it is sacred privilege.

Intercessors who lose reverence lose accuracy.

Recognizing When You Have Entered This Realm

How does an intercessor know they have entered the Holy of Holies?

- The atmosphere becomes weighty
- Words decrease
- Awareness sharpens
- Instruction becomes clear
- Peace settles, even in urgency

This is where intercession becomes precise.

The Role of the Blood of Jesus

Scripture teaches that access to the Holy of Holies is granted through the blood of Jesus:

"Having therefore, brethren, boldness to enter into the holiest by the blood of Jesus..." (Hebrews 10:19, KJV)

Intercessors do not enter through effort or emotion—but through covenant.

Confidence in prayer flows from understanding redemption.

Why This Realm Is Not for Performance

The Holy of Holies cannot be performed. It cannot be rushed. It cannot be shared publicly. It is private, weighty, and sacred.

Intercessors who crave affirmation will struggle here. This realm requires maturity.

God trains intercessors here because this is where obedience is tested.

When Intercessors Refuse to Bow

Pride is subtle in prayer. It manifests as constant speaking, resistance to silence, and refusal to yield control.

The Holy of Holies demands bowing—not physically, but internally.

God resists pride even in prayer.

A Call to Discipline

Entering the Holy of Holies requires discipline. Intercessors must practice:

- Stillness
- Listening
- Restraint
- Obedience
- Confidentiality

These disciplines preserve authority.

Why Many Prayer Gatherings Never Reach This Realm

Group prayer often remains in outer courts because silence feels uncomfortable. Leaders fear losing momentum. Intercessors fear inactivity.

But momentum without instruction is spiritual motion without destination.

Prayer leaders must be courageous enough to lead people into silence.

The Shift That Changes Everything

When intercessors learn to enter the Holy of Holies, prayer changes. Words become fewer. Authority increases. Fatigue decreases. Clarity sharpens.

This realm is where intercessors stop reacting and start responding.

Pray This

Father, take me beyond surface prayer. Teach me to bow before I speak. Silence my flesh and sharpen my spirit. I desire Your instruction more than expression. I choose reverence over routine and obedience over emotion.

When This Happens... Pray Like This

When you feel pressure to perform in prayer:

"Lord, quiet my soul so I can hear You clearly."

Declarations

- I enter the Holy of Holies with reverence.
- I hear before I speak.
- I pray from posture, not pressure.
- I steward revelation with discipline.

Activation

Spend ten minutes in silence before prayer. Write down what the Holy Spirit impresses on you. Pray only what He reveals—nothing more.

Footnotes

1. Andrew Murray, With Christ in the School of Prayer (New Kensington, PA: Whitaker House, 1981), 61–72.
2. E. M. Bounds, Power Through Prayer (Grand Rapids: Baker Books, 1991), 53–60.
3. Derek Prince, Shaping History Through Prayer and Fasting (Old Tappan, NJ: Chosen Books, 1997), 93–101.
4. Watchman Nee, The Authority of the Believer (New York: Christian Fellowship Publishers, 1972), 123–136.
5. Gordon D. Fee, God's Empowering Presence (Peabody, MA: Hendrickson, 1994), 895–903.

CHAPTER 4
HE IS CALLING US HIGHER

There is a consistent pattern in Scripture: when God wants to protect people on the ground, He elevates intercessors in the spirit. Elevation is not about status—it is about vision. The higher God brings an intercessor, the clearer they can see what others cannot yet perceive.

This chapter addresses a call that many intercessors feel but do not always understand:

God is calling us higher—not emotionally, but positionally.

Spiritual elevation is not excitement; it is responsibility. To come higher means to see earlier, discern faster, and respond more accurately. God does not elevate intercessors for personal encounters alone—He elevates them so they can guard destinies, intercept attacks, and steward insight.

Elevation Changes Perspective

Remaining on ground level limits vision. When intercessors pray only from their immediate circumstances, emotions dominate interpretation. Fear feels larger. Pressure feels heavier. Confusion feels closer.

But elevation changes the frame.

"If ye then be risen with Christ, seek those things which are above... Set your affection on things above, not on things on the earth." (Colossians 3:1–2, KJV)

To seek what is above is to adopt heaven's vantage point. From above, patterns become visible. Timing becomes clearer. What once felt overwhelming begins to look manageable.

God calls intercessors higher because threats are often recognized from elevation, not proximity.

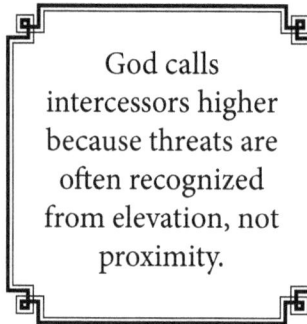

God calls intercessors higher because threats are often recognized from elevation, not proximity.

Higher Does Not Mean Removed

One of the misunderstandings about spiritual elevation is the belief that coming higher disconnects intercessors from earthly realities. The opposite is true. Elevation brings clarity, not detachment.

Jesus consistently operated from a heavenly perspective while remaining fully engaged with earthly need. He saw sickness before others named it. He perceived resistance before it surfaced. He responded before crisis escalated.

Elevation does not make intercessors aloof—it makes them accurate.

The Invitation to "Come Up"

Throughout Scripture, God invites His servants upward when He is preparing to reveal something significant:

- Moses was called up the mountain before receiving instruction.
- John was told, "Come up hither," before receiving revelation (Revelation 4:1).
- Ezekiel was lifted by the Spirit to see what others could not perceive.

Elevation always precedes revelation.

God calls intercessors higher because He intends to show them something that cannot be discerned from ground level.

Why Many Resist Elevation

Elevation requires leaving familiarity. It requires letting go of emotional dependence on affirmation, noise, and movement. Higher places often feel quieter, lonelier, and weightier.

Some intercessors resist elevation because:

- Silence feels uncomfortable
- Responsibility feels heavy
- Accountability increases
- Visibility decreases

Higher realms are not crowded. They are disciplined.

But God does not elevate to isolate—He elevates to entrust.

Seeing Before Evidence Appears

One of the clearest indicators that an intercessor has been called higher is the ability to sense danger before there is proof. God often reveals what is forming long before it manifests.

"Surely the Lord GOD will do nothing, but he revealeth his secret unto his servants the prophets." (Amos 3:7, KJV)

Intercessors often feel urgency without explanation. This is not anxiety—it is insight. When elevation increases, warning systems sharpen.

The tragedy occurs when intercessors dismiss this awareness because there is "no evidence yet." By the time evidence appears, the opportunity for interception may already be lost.

Discernment Over Drama

Elevation produces discernment, not dramatics. Intercessors who operate from higher perspective do not panic easily. They do not exaggerate. They do not react impulsively.

They intercept calmly.

The enemy thrives on reaction. Heaven responds through discernment.

Intercessors called higher learn to separate emotional alarm from spiritual alert. One produces fear; the other produces action.

Why God Elevates Before Attacks Escalate

Many intercessors wonder why God allows them to sense pressure early. The answer is simple: prevention is more effective than repair.

God does not wait for destruction to occur before He responds—He reveals forming threats to trained intercessors who know how to pray strategically.

Elevation is not about experiencing more—it is about preventing loss.

The Cost of Remaining Low

Intercessors who refuse elevation remain vulnerable to distraction, fatigue, and emotional overload. Ground-level prayer reacts to symptoms. Elevated prayer addresses sources.

Remaining low keeps intercessors busy but ineffective.

God is calling intercessors to stop praying from within the problem and start praying over it.

Perspective Produces Authority

Authority flows from alignment with heaven's perspective. When intercessors see what God sees, they speak what God speaks—and heaven backs it.

Jesus operated with authority because He only spoke what He heard the Father say (John 5:19). Elevation produces restraint.

Intercessors who speak less often carry more weight.

Elevated Intercession Requires Emotional Maturity

Coming higher requires emotional regulation. Intercessors must learn to process emotion without being governed by it. Elevated spaces expose insecurity, fear, and the need for validation.

God addresses these issues because unchecked emotion distorts discernment.

Elevation refines the intercessor before it releases authority.

Why Not Everyone Is Called Higher at the Same Time

God elevates according to readiness, not desire. Elevation requires trustworthiness. Those who mishandle insight, over-spiritualize impressions, or speak prematurely are often kept lower until maturity develops.

Elevation is not favoritism—it is stewardship.

Staying Higher Requires Discipline

Elevation is not a moment—it is a maintained posture. Intercessors must practice:

- Daily consecration
- Scriptural grounding
- Emotional discipline
- Confidentiality
- Obedience to instruction

Without discipline, elevation becomes dangerous.

A Word to Those Feeling the Pull

If you feel a consistent pull to go higher—to pray differently, to listen longer, to respond more precisely—that pull is not imagination. It is invitation.

God is not calling you away from people—He is calling you above the noise so you can protect them more effectively.

Pray This

Father, lift my perspective. Take me higher than emotion, fear, and reaction. Teach me to see from where You sit. Train my eyes to recognize what is forming and my heart to respond with obedience. I accept the responsibility that comes with elevation.

When This Happens... Pray Like This

When you sense danger before evidence appears:

"Lord, I intercept this assignment now. Show me how to respond accurately and quietly."

Declarations

- I accept God's invitation to come higher.
- I see before the enemy strikes.
- I respond with discernment, not fear.
- I steward elevated insight responsibly.

Activation

Ask the Holy Spirit to reveal one area where He is calling you higher in intercession. Write it down. Ask what discipline or adjustment is required to remain there.

Footnotes

1. Andrew Murray, With Christ in the School of Prayer (New Kensington, PA: Whitaker House, 1981), 73–84.
2. E. M. Bounds, Power Through Prayer (Grand Rapids: Baker Books, 1991), 61–68.
3. Dutch Sheets, Intercessory Prayer (Ventura, CA: Regal Books, 1996), 119–136.
4. Derek Prince, Shaping History Through Prayer and Fasting (Old Tappan, NJ: Chosen Books, 1997), 103–111.
5. Watchman Nee, The Authority of the Believer (New York: Christian Fellowship Publishers, 1972), 137–151.

PART II
TRAINING THE
INTERCESSOR

CHAPTER 5
INTIMACY WITH THE HOLY SPIRIT

Intercessory prayer cannot be sustained without intimacy with the Holy Spirit. Strategy flows from relationship. Accuracy flows from communion. Endurance flows from obedience. Without intimacy, intercession becomes mechanical, reactive, and exhausting. With intimacy, intercession becomes responsive, disciplined, and effective.

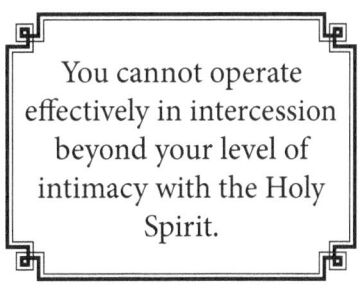

You cannot operate effectively in intercession beyond your level of intimacy with the Holy Spirit.

This chapter addresses a truth that must be settled in every intercessor:

You cannot operate effectively in intercession beyond your level of intimacy with the Holy Spirit.

Spiritual authority is not rooted in knowledge alone. It is rooted in proximity. Intercessors who hear clearly do so because they remain close. Those who respond accurately do so because they have learned the Spirit's voice, timing, and urgency.

Intimacy Is Not Familiarity

One of the greatest misconceptions in prayer culture is the confusion between intimacy and familiarity. Familiarity assumes access without reverence. Intimacy preserves closeness while honoring holiness.

The Holy Spirit is not a concept to be studied—He is a Person to be known. Intercessors must move beyond interacting with the Spirit only during prayer gatherings and develop daily sensitivity to His presence.

Jesus promised this relationship:

"Howbeit when he, the Spirit of truth, is come, he will guide you into all truth… and he will shew you things to come." (John 16:13, KJV)

Guidance requires trust. Trust is built through consistent intimacy.

Why Intimacy Determines Timing

Intercession is often time-sensitive. Delayed obedience can weaken or even nullify effectiveness. When the Holy Spirit prompts an intercessor to pray now, it is because something is forming in real time.

Intimacy sharpens urgency.

Intercessors who walk closely with the Holy Spirit learn to recognize the difference between general burden and immediate instruction. They sense when prayer can wait—and when it cannot.

Delayed response is often not rebellion; it is unfamiliarity with the Spirit's voice.

Sensitivity Over Schedule

Intimacy with the Holy Spirit disrupts rigid scheduling. While discipline is essential, intimacy teaches flexibility. The Spirit may prompt prayer in the middle of the night, during ordinary activities, or in moments that feel inconvenient.

Intercessors who insist on praying only on schedule may miss assignments entirely.

The Spirit speaks when danger is forming—not when calendars permit.

Obedience Sustains Authority

Authority is maintained through obedience. Each time an intercessor responds promptly to the Holy Spirit, sensitivity increases. Each time obedience is delayed, clarity dulls.

Scripture affirms this connection:

"Grieve not the holy Spirit of God, whereby ye are sealed unto the day of redemption." (Ephesians 4:30, KJV)

Grief occurs not only through sin, but through consistent resistance to promptings. Intimacy requires attentiveness.

Why Intercessors Must Learn the Spirit's Language

The Holy Spirit often communicates through impressions, urgency, stillness, scripture recall, or subtle discomfort. Intercessors who expect dramatic signals may miss quiet instructions.

Intimacy trains discernment.

Intercessors must learn how the Spirit communicates with them personally. Comparison disrupts clarity. What feels urgent to one may feel gentle to another—but obedience remains the standard.

Intimacy Guards Against Burnout

Many intercessors burn out not because they pray too much—but because they pray disconnected from the Spirit's rhythm. Intimacy teaches when to engage and when to rest.

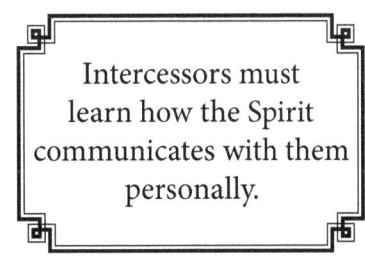

Intercessors must learn how the Spirit communicates with them personally.

The Holy Spirit does not exhaust intercessors—He sustains them.

"But the Lord is faithful, who shall stablish you, and keep you from evil." (2 Thessalonians 3:3, KJV)

When intercessors pray without intimacy, they rely on emotional energy. When they pray with intimacy, they draw from divine strength.

Responding to Night Watches and Sudden Urgency

One of the marks of deep intimacy is responsiveness during night watches. Many intercessors experience sudden awakenings without explanation. These moments are often assignments.

Intimacy teaches intercessors not to ignore these moments.

Scripture reveals night watches as significant times of intercession. God often interrupts rest to preserve life.

Ignoring these prompts dulls sensitivity. Responding sharpens it.

Intimacy Requires Trusting the Spirit Over Logic

The Holy Spirit often prompts prayer without providing full explanation. Intercessors must trust that obedience precedes understanding.

Waiting for clarity before obedience often results in missed timing.

Intimacy means trusting the Spirit's leading even when logic resists.

Why Disobedience Weakens Discernment

Repeated hesitation dulls spiritual hearing. The Spirit does not force compliance—He invites partnership. Over time, ignored promptings become quieter.

Intercessors must guard responsiveness.

Obedience keeps communication clear.

Intimacy and Emotional Discipline

Intercessors with intimacy learn to process emotion without being governed by it. The Holy Spirit stabilizes emotional fluctuations and prevents overreaction.

Emotion informs—but intimacy governs.

Intercessors must learn to bring emotion into submission rather than allowing it to lead prayer.

Living a Spirit-Led Life Beyond Prayer Time

Intimacy with the Holy Spirit is not reserved for prayer gatherings. It is cultivated through daily obedience, repentance, and attentiveness.

Intercessors who ignore the Spirit in daily life will struggle to hear Him clearly in prayer.

Lifestyle intimacy sustains prayer authority.

The Holy Spirit as Intercessor

Scripture teaches that the Holy Spirit Himself intercedes:

"Likewise the Spirit also helpeth our infirmities… maketh intercession for us with groanings which cannot be uttered." (Romans 8:26, KJV)

Intercessors partner with the Spirit—they do not replace Him. Intimacy allows alignment with His intercession rather than striving independently.

Why Intimacy Protects Accuracy

Intercessors without intimacy may misinterpret impressions. Intimacy provides context. The Spirit confirms, redirects, and refines prayer.

Accuracy flows from relationship.

A Call to Consistent Communion

This chapter calls intercessors to deepen relationship, not increase activity. Intimacy requires time, humility, and attentiveness.

God is not impressed by busy intercessors—He is pleased by responsive ones.

Pray This

Holy Spirit, I desire intimacy with You more than productivity. Train my ears to recognize Your voice and my heart to respond without delay. Interrupt me when necessary. Wake me when needed. I choose obedience over comfort and sensitivity over routine.

When This Happens... Pray Like This

When you sense urgency without explanation:

"Holy Spirit, I respond now. Show me how to pray accurately and briefly."

Declarations

- I walk in intimacy with the Holy Spirit.
- I respond quickly to His promptings.
- I am sensitive, obedient, and accurate.
- I do not delay when the Spirit speaks.

Activation

For the next seven days, journal every prompting you sense from the Holy Spirit and how you respond. Ask Him to refine your sensitivity.

Footnotes

1. Gordon D. Fee, God's Empowering Presence: The Holy Spirit in the Letters of Paul (Peabody, MA: Hendrickson, 1994), 903–915.
2. Andrew Murray, With Christ in the School of Prayer (New Kensington, PA: Whitaker House, 1981), 85–96.
3. E. M. Bounds, Power Through Prayer (Grand Rapids: Baker Books, 1991), 69–77.
4. Derek Prince, Shaping History Through Prayer and Fasting (Old Tappan, NJ: Chosen Books, 1997), 113–121.
5. Dutch Sheets, Intercessory Prayer (Ventura, CA: Regal Books, 1996), 137–149.

CHAPTER 6
THE SITUATION ROOM

Intercessors do not operate in chaos. They operate in order.

This chapter introduces one of the most critical identity shifts an intercessor must embrace: intercession is heaven's situation room on earth. When intercessors understand this, prayer is no longer casual, reactive, or emotional—it becomes disciplined, strategic, and authoritative.

A situation room exists for one purpose: to monitor threats, receive intelligence, assess risk, and determine response. No one enters casually. No one speaks unnecessarily. No one operates emotionally. Every word matters because lives, systems, and futures are at stake.

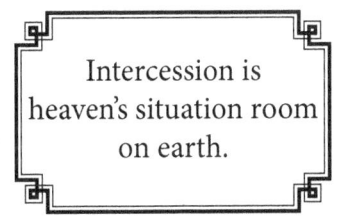

Intercession is heaven's situation room on earth.

God designed intercession to function the same way.

Why God Reveals Intelligence to Intercessors

One of the most misunderstood aspects of intercession is revelation. Many intercessors assume that when God shows them something, it is for discussion, warning, or exposure. Scripture teaches the opposite.

God reveals so intercessors can pray, not so they can speak.

"Surely the Lord GOD will do nothing, but he revealeth his secret unto his servants the prophets." (Amos 3:7, KJV)

Revelation is not permission to announce—it is instruction to intercede. Spiritual intelligence is given so assignments can be intercepted before they manifest. When revelation is mishandled, trust is broken.

God entrusts information only to those who will steward it responsibly.

The Discipline of the Situation Room

In a natural situation room, discipline is non-negotiable. Conversations are measured. Information is guarded. Responses are deliberate. Emotional reactions are dangerous.

Intercessors must adopt the same discipline.

Prayer gatherings that function as emotional free-for-alls are not situation rooms—they are release chambers. While emotional release may feel good, it rarely produces strategic outcomes.

The situation room requires restraint.

Intercessors must learn when to speak, when to listen, and when to remain silent.

Watchmen on the Wall

Scripture consistently identifies intercessors as watchmen.

"I have set watchmen upon thy walls, O Jerusalem, which shall never hold their peace day nor night." (Isaiah 62:6, KJV)

Watchmen do not sleep on duty. They do not become distracted. They do not ignore subtle shifts. Their responsibility is vigilance.

A watchman who misses a signal endangers everyone behind the wall.

Intercessors in the situation room must maintain spiritual alertness. Complacency is dangerous.

Confidentiality Is Not Optional

One of the greatest tests of maturity for an intercessor is confidentiality. God often reveals sensitive matters involving leaders, families, churches, regions, and destinies. These revelations are not meant to be shared—they are meant to be covered.

Talking about what God reveals weakens protection.

Intercessors who cannot guard information cannot be trusted with more.

Confidentiality preserves authority.

Why God Does Not Reveal Everything to Everyone

God reveals strategically. Not every intercessor receives the same information. Roles differ. Assignments differ. Levels of trust differ.

Some intercessors are watchers.

Some are gap-standers.

Some are warfare responders.

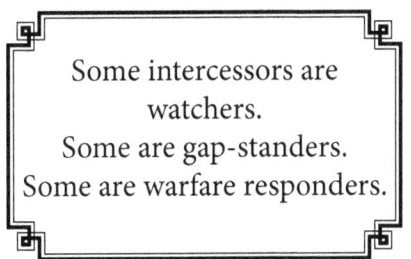

Some intercessors are watchers. Some are gap-standers. Some are warfare responders.

Confusion occurs when intercessors attempt to operate outside their assigned function.

The situation room functions effectively because every role is clear.

Emotional Regulation in the Situation Room

Emotion is information—but it must be regulated.

In a natural situation room, panic leads to mistakes. The same is true spiritually. Intercessors must learn to feel urgency without reacting emotionally.

Calm does not mean passive. Calm means controlled authority.

The Holy Spirit does not produce chaos—He produces clarity.

When God Sounds the Alarm

Not every moment in the situation room carries the same intensity. Some seasons require monitoring. Others require immediate response.

Intercessors must learn to discern levels of threat—a concept that will be explored deeply in the DEFCON chapter. For now, understand this: urgency does not always require noise.

Sometimes the most urgent moments require silence, listening, and precise instruction.

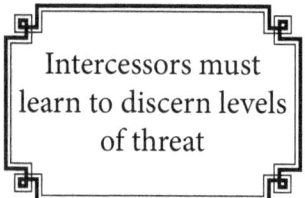

Intercessors must learn to discern levels of threat

Why Silence Is Critical in the Situation Room

Silence allows information to surface. Noise often covers it.

God often reveals strategy in quiet moments—after worship subsides, after emotion settles, after voices are stilled.

Intercessors who rush to speak often miss instruction.

Silence is not inactivity—it is readiness.

Prayer Before Conversation

One of the governing rules of the situation room is this: pray before you speak.

If God reveals something concerning, sensitive, or urgent, the first response must be prayer—not discussion, not speculation, not warning others prematurely.

Prayer stabilizes situations before words ever could.

Guarding Spiritual Intelligence

Spiritual intelligence must be guarded against:

- Gossip
- Assumption

- Fear-based interpretation
- Premature action

Intercessors must submit revelation back to God before responding. This preserves clarity and prevents missteps.

Authority Is Exercised, Not Announced

Intercessors do not announce authority—they enforce it.

Authority does not require explanation. It requires alignment.

The situation room is not a place to prove spirituality—it is a place to execute assignment.

Why Some Intercessors Feel Isolated

Intercessors often feel isolated because of the confidentiality required in their assignment. They cannot share what they carry. They cannot explain urgency. They cannot broadcast burden.

This isolation is not punishment—it is protection.

God often separates intercessors so they can remain focused.

A Warning About Mishandling Revelation

Scripture warns against careless speech. When intercessors speak prematurely, they often create fear, confusion, or resistance.

God expects restraint.

Revelation spoken too soon can become accusation instead of protection.

The Weight of Trust

Being invited into the situation room is a mark of trust. God does not reveal sensitive information to untrained or undisciplined intercessors.

Trust increases with faithfulness.

When intercessors prove they can guard what God reveals, He entrusts them with more.

Training the Intercessor for the Situation Room

Intercessors must be trained to:

- Listen more than speak
- Guard information carefully
- Respond strategically
- Maintain emotional discipline
- Remain alert over long periods

This training does not happen overnight. It is cultivated through obedience and humility.

Why This Chapter Matters

Without understanding the situation room, intercessors misinterpret revelation, mishandle urgency, and exhaust themselves unnecessarily.

This chapter redefines intercession as strategic responsibility, not emotional reaction.

Pray This

Father, thank You for trusting intercessors with spiritual intelligence. Train me to guard what You reveal. Teach me to listen carefully, respond accurately, and remain disciplined. I choose prayer over conversation and obedience over impulse.

When This Happens… Pray Like This

When God reveals something sensitive:

"Lord, I cover this in prayer. Show me how to respond quietly and effectively."

Declarations

- I am a trusted watchman.
- I guard spiritual intelligence responsibly.
- I pray before I speak.
- I respond with clarity and authority.

Activation

Commit to taking every piece of spiritual insight directly to prayer before sharing it with anyone. Ask the Holy Spirit to confirm when—and if—it should be spoken.

Footnotes

1. Dutch Sheets, Intercessory Prayer (Ventura, CA: Regal Books, 1996), 151–168.
2. E. M. Bounds, Power Through Prayer (Grand Rapids: Baker Books, 1991), 79–86.
3. Andrew Murray, With Christ in the School of Prayer (New Kensington, PA: Whitaker House, 1981), 97–108.
4. Derek Prince, Shaping History Through Prayer and Fasting (Old Tappan, NJ: Chosen Books, 1997), 123–131.
5. Watchman Nee, The Authority of the Believer (New York: Christian Fellowship Publishers, 1972), 153–167.

CHAPTER 7
WHY INTERCESSORS NEED ASSIGNMENTS

Intercessors were never meant to pray about everything. They were meant to pray according to assignment.

This chapter confronts one of the most common and damaging misconceptions in intercessory prayer: the belief that spiritual maturity is measured by how much one can carry. In truth, unassigned prayer does not increase authority—it dilutes it. Many intercessors burn out not because they pray too much, but because they pray without focus.

Assignment is not limitation.

Assignment is protection.

God assigns intercessors because He is strategic. Heaven does nothing randomly, and intercession is no exception.

The Cost of Unassigned Intercession

When intercessors pray without assignment, several things begin to happen:

- Prayer becomes scattered and exhausting
- Burdens multiply without resolution
- Emotional fatigue replaces spiritual clarity
- Authority weakens due to lack of focus

Unassigned intercession often feels urgent but unclear. Intercessors feel pulled in multiple directions, responding to every need, crisis, or headline. Over time, this produces frustration and discouragement.

God never intended intercessors to carry the weight of the world.

Assignment Clarifies Responsibility

Assignment answers critical questions before prayer begins:

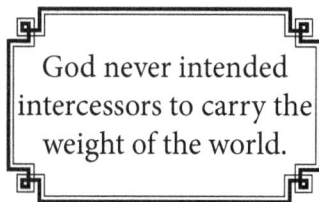

God never intended intercessors to carry the weight of the world.

- *What am I responsible for?*
- *What am I not responsible for?*
- *Where has God authorized me to stand?*
- *What requires my attention right now?*

Without answers to these questions, intercessors often overextend themselves, assuming responsibility God never gave.

Scripture teaches that God assigns intentionally:

"I sought for a man among them, that should make up the hedge, and stand in the gap before me..." (Ezekiel 22:30, KJV)

God did not seek everyone—He sought a man. Assignment narrows focus so authority can be concentrated.

Why Carrying Everything Weakens Authority

Authority flows through obedience, not effort. When intercessors attempt to pray for everything, they step outside obedience and into presumption.

God honors prayers aligned with assignment because they reflect listening.

Praying beyond assignment often feels noble—but it is unsustainable.

Assignment preserves strength so intercessors can remain faithful over time.

Assignment Is a Sign of Trust

God assigns intercessors because He trusts them. Assignment indicates that heaven has assessed capacity, maturity, and reliability.

Assignment is not given to impress—it is given to protect.

God does not assign what an intercessor cannot steward.

Biblical Examples of Assignment

Scripture consistently demonstrates assignment in intercession:

- Moses was assigned to Israel, not Egypt
- Samuel was assigned to hear God for the nation
- Daniel was assigned to pray for Jerusalem's restoration
- Esther was assigned to stand in the gap for her people

None of these intercessors carried everything. They carried what God assigned—and history shifted.

Assignment Sharpens Discernment

When assignment is clear, discernment becomes sharper. Intercessors learn to recognize what is relevant and what is distraction.

Without assignment, everything feels urgent.

Assignment teaches intercessors to say no without guilt.

God does not assign what an intercessor cannot steward.

The Danger of Emotional Assignment

Some intercessors assign themselves based on emotional connection rather than divine instruction. While compassion is vital, emotion alone is not authorization.

Praying from emotional attachment without assignment often leads to over-identification and fatigue.

Assignment brings objectivity.

Why Assignment Preserves Longevity

God designs intercession for endurance, not short bursts of intensity. Assignment protects intercessors from burnout by limiting scope and preserving strength.

Intercessors who remain unassigned often withdraw entirely after seasons of exhaustion.

Assignment sustains longevity.

Roles Within Assignment

Assignment often aligns with function. Some intercessors are:

- Watchers – discerning shifts and warning of danger
- Gap-standers – covering leaders, families, or regions
- Warfare intercessors – confronting resistance directly
- Stabilizers – maintaining peace and order during crisis

Confusion occurs when intercessors attempt to function outside their grace.

Unity does not require sameness—it requires alignment.

When Assignment Changes

Assignments are seasonal. God may shift focus as seasons change. Intercessors must remain flexible and attentive.

Clinging to expired assignments creates frustration.

Assignment requires continual listening.

The Relationship Between Assignment and Authority

Authority increases where assignment is honored. When intercessors stay within their lane, prayers carry weight and clarity.

Authority weakens when assignment is ignored.

Jesus modeled this perfectly—He only did what He saw the Father doing (John 5:19).

Group Intercession and Assignment

Corporate prayer must also operate by assignment. Prayer leaders should define focus before prayer begins.

Agreement amplifies authority.

Unfocused group prayer often results in spiritual noise without outcome.

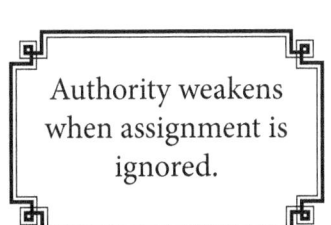

Authority weakens when assignment is ignored.

Recognizing Your Assignment

Assignment is often confirmed through:

- Consistent burden in one area
- Repeated confirmation through Scripture
- Fruitfulness over time
- Peace rather than pressure

Assignment does not produce chaos—it produces clarity.

Assignment Is Stewardship

God evaluates faithfulness, not volume. Intercessors will give account for how they stewarded what was assigned—not for what they attempted beyond instruction.

Assignment teaches restraint.

A Warning Against Comparison

Comparing assignments creates insecurity. God assigns differently based on calling and capacity.

Assignment is personal.

Comparison weakens confidence and clarity.

A Call to Release What Is Not Assigned

Intercessors must learn to release burdens God did not assign. Carrying unnecessary weight does not honor God—it exhausts the intercessor.

Release is obedience.

Pray This

Father, clarify my assignment. Remove the need to carry what You have not given me. Teach me to steward my responsibility with discipline and faithfulness. I choose obedience over overwhelm.

When This Happens… Pray Like This

When you feel pulled in too many directions:

"Lord, narrow my focus and align me with what You have assigned."

Declarations

- I am assigned, not scattered.
- I steward my responsibility faithfully.
- I release what God has not given me.
- My assignment carries authority.

Activation

Ask the Holy Spirit to clearly define one intercessory assignment you are responsible for in this season. Write it down. Commit to pray consistently and specifically for that assignment only.

Footnotes

1. Derek Prince, Shaping History Through Prayer and Fasting (Old Tappan, NJ: Chosen Books, 1997), 133–141.
2. Dutch Sheets, Intercessory Prayer (Ventura, CA: Regal Books, 1996), 171–189.
3. E. M. Bounds, Power Through Prayer (Grand Rapids: Baker Books, 1991), 87–94.
4. Andrew Murray, With Christ in the School of Prayer (New Kensington, PA: Whitaker House, 1981), 109–121.
5. Watchman Nee, The Authority of the Believer (New York: Christian Fellowship Publishers, 1972), 169–182.

CHAPTER 8
DEFCON INTERCESSION LEVELS

God does not respond to every moment the same way—and neither should intercessors.

That truth alone dismantles one of the most common errors in modern prayer culture: the assumption that intensity equals accuracy. Too often, intercessors approach every prayer moment with the same posture, the same emotional tone, and the same language, regardless of what is actually occurring in the spirit. They cry when command is required. They worship when warfare is forming. They shout when silence would release strategy. They hesitate when authority is demanded.

Intercessory prayer is not uniform. It is discerning.

This chapter introduces a framework God used to train us in discernment—what I call DEFCON Intercession Levels. This language did not come from military study or trend analysis. It came through revelation, as God taught us that not every prayer moment carries the same weight, urgency, or required response. Misreading the moment in intercession can cost protection, delay intervention, and weaken authority.

Discernment Determines Response

Scripture repeatedly teaches that discernment precedes effective action. The sons of Issachar were commended not because of their strength, but because they "had understanding of the times, to know what Israel ought to do."[1] Intercession functions the same way. Heaven expects intercessors to recognize what time it is in the spirit before responding.

Uniform prayer weakens authority because it ignores timing. Strategic intercession, by contrast, responds to threat level, formation, and urgency. This principle is consistent throughout Scripture and historic intercessory theology. As Dutch Sheets explains, effective intercession is "the ability to hear what heaven is saying about earth and then pray it into manifestation."[2]

The Revelation Behind DEFCON Intercession

The concept of DEFCON became clear to me while observing how threat assessment works in the natural realm. In national security, DEFCON levels exist to prevent panic, preserve life, and ensure accurate response. Each level dictates posture, urgency, and action. No one in a situation room responds emotionally. They respond strategically.

The Holy Spirit impressed this truth deeply: this is how intercessors are supposed to pray.

Intercessors are heaven's responders on earth. They are not called to react emotionally but to respond discerningly. Scripture affirms that God reveals information in advance so that His servants can respond appropriately.[3] Revelation without response is incomplete. Response without discernment is dangerous.

DEFCON 5: Peaceful Monitoring and Listening

DEFCON 5 represents a posture of peace, not passivity. This is the level where there is no immediate threat, but spiritual awareness must remain active. Many intercessors misunderstand peace as permission to disengage. In reality, peace is often the environment where God whispers future instruction.

At this level, intercession looks like worship, listening, and attentiveness. The intercessor remains positioned, not idle. Scripture consistently links stillness with spiritual awareness:

"Be still, and know that I am God." (Psalm 46:10, KJV)

Andrew Murray emphasizes that stillness before God is not inactivity but readiness, training the soul to receive divine instruction rather than generate human effort.[4] DEFCON 5 intercession gathers intelligence. It prepares the intercessor for what may come without creating unnecessary urgency.

DEFCON 4: Heightened Awareness

DEFCON 4 indicates that something has shifted. There may be no visible evidence, but the atmosphere feels altered. Distractions increase. Resistance subtly rises. The intercessor senses alertness rather than alarm.

Jesus instructed His disciples to "watch and pray," not panic and pray.[5] Watching comes first. At this level, prayer becomes preventative. Intercessors pray protectively—covering minds, relationships, leadership, and decision-making before the enemy gains access.

Derek Prince notes that much spiritual warfare is lost simply because believers respond too late, after footholds have already been established.[6] DEFCON 4 intercession exists to prevent escalation.

DEFCON 3: Formation of Threat

DEFCON 3 is where pressure becomes tangible. The intercessor senses weight that is no longer subtle. Emotional agitation may rise, but the trained intercessor does not confuse agitation with instruction.

This is the stage where discernment must mature into strategy.

Scripture teaches that the enemy often forms plans before manifesting them, and God responds by raising a standard through His Spirit.[7] At DEFCON 3, intercessors pray specifically. They identify access points. They apply Scripture intentionally. They resist formation before manifestation.

E. M. Bounds reminds us that prayer is most effective when it is focused, deliberate, and rooted in spiritual authority rather than emotional intensity.[8]

DEFCON 2: Active Assignment

DEFCON 2 signals that the threat is no longer theoretical—it is operational. This is the realm of active warfare. Prayer at this level is authoritative, restrained, and unwavering.

This is not the time for vague language or emotional expression. Authority replaces conversation. Scripture affirms that believers have been given authority over the power of the enemy, not merely permission to plead.[9]

God trusts intercessors who can read seasons.

Watchman Nee emphasizes that authority in prayer is exercised, not explained.[10] Intercessors at DEFCON 2 dismantle, cancel, restrain, and forbid with confidence rooted in covenant. They pray knowing who they are and whose authority they carry.

DEFCON 1: Life-or-Death Intercession

DEFCON 1 represents emergency intercession. Lives, destinies, callings, or spiritual futures are at stake. This is where endurance is required. Intercessors may experience travail, urgency, or prolonged burden—not because emotion is leading, but because standing is required.

Scripture describes this kind of intercession as standing in the gap.[11] It is not dramatic. It is faithful. DEFCON 1 intercession continues until God releases peace, instruction, or breakthrough.

Dutch Sheets describes this level of intercession as "staying until heaven answers," noting that premature withdrawal often leaves assignments incomplete.[12]

Learning to Shift Levels

The maturity of an intercessor is revealed not by how intensely they pray, but by how accurately they shift. Remaining at DEFCON 5 when DEFCON 2 is required leads to loss. Remaining at DEFCON 1 when peace has returned leads to burnout.

God trusts intercessors who can read seasons.

Intercession is not reaction. It is response.

A Call to Discernment

This chapter calls intercessors out of emotional sameness into spiritual intelligence. God is not seeking louder prayers—He is seeking trained watchmen who know how to respond to the moment.

Intercessors who understand levels do not panic. They discern. They do not guess. They respond. And because of that, lives are preserved, attacks are intercepted, and heaven's will is enforced quietly and effectively.

Footnotes

1. 1 Chronicles 12:32 (KJV).
2. Dutch Sheets, Intercessory Prayer (Ventura, CA: Regal Books, 1996), 45–47.
3. Amos 3:7 (KJV).
4. Andrew Murray, With Christ in the School of Prayer (New Kensington, PA: Whitaker House, 1981), 112–118.
5. Matthew 26:41 (KJV).
6. Derek Prince, Shaping History Through Prayer and Fasting (Old Tappan, NJ: Chosen Books, 1997), 84–88.
7. Isaiah 59:19 (KJV).
8. E. M. Bounds, Power Through Prayer (Grand Rapids: Baker Books, 1991), 92–99.
9. Luke 10:19 (KJV).
10. Watchman Nee, The Authority of the Believer (New York: Christian Fellowship Publishers, 1972), 55–63.
11. Ezekiel 22:30 (KJV).
12. Dutch Sheets, Intercessory Prayer, 171–176.

PART III
RESPONSIBILITY AND ENDURANCE

CHAPTER 9
ROLES WITHIN THE INTERCESSOR SITUATION ROOM

Every effective situation room functions because everyone inside understands their role. Confusion of function creates delay. Competition creates distraction. Disorder creates vulnerability. The same is true in intercession.

One of the most common reasons prayer environments lose authority is not lack of passion, prayer time, or sincerity—it is role confusion. When intercessors do not understand how God has positioned them, they attempt to operate outside their grace. What results is overlap, exhaustion, frustration, and, in some cases, spiritual interference rather than spiritual coverage.

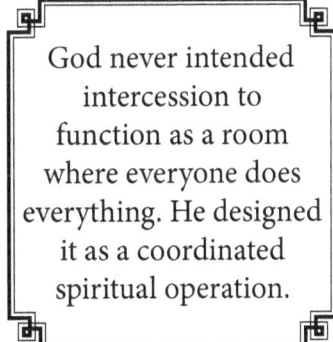

God never intended intercession to function as a room where everyone does everything. He designed it as a coordinated spiritual operation.

God never intended intercession to function as a room where everyone does everything. He designed it as a coordinated spiritual operation.

Unity Does Not Mean Sameness

Scripture is clear that unity in the Body of Christ does not require sameness of function. The apostle Paul emphasizes that God places members in the body "as it hath pleased him," not according to personal preference or perceived importance.[1] Intercessors are no different. God assigns roles intentionally, and when those roles are honored, authority flows freely.

Problems arise when intercessors believe maturity is proven by doing what someone else is doing. When comparison enters the situation room, discernment exits. Unity is not achieved when everyone sounds alike—it is achieved when everyone functions in alignment.

Why Roles Exist in Intercession

Roles exist because intercession deals with layered realities. Some moments require early detection. Others require sustained coverage. Others demand confrontation. Still others require stabilization after conflict. One intercessor cannot effectively carry all of these functions simultaneously.

God assigns roles to preserve clarity.

This pattern is evident throughout Scripture. In the rebuilding of Jerusalem, some guarded the wall, some carried materials, and some stood ready to defend.[2] The success of the mission depended on role clarity, not equal activity.

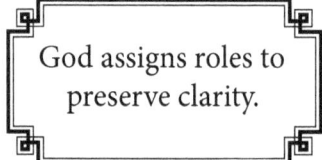

God assigns roles to preserve clarity.

Intercession works the same way.

Watchers: Those Who Discern Shifts

Some intercessors are watchers. They are highly sensitive to atmosphere, timing, and spiritual movement. They often discern shifts before others feel them. Their role is not always to pray loudly or at length, but to notice, interpret, and alert.

Watchers are often misunderstood because they speak less and observe more. But Scripture honors this role deeply. God consistently sets watchmen to perceive danger and respond before destruction arrives.[3]

When watchers attempt to become warriors prematurely, or when their discernment is dismissed, the situation room loses early-warning capability.

Gap-Standers: Those Who Cover Consistently

Other intercessors are gap-standers. They carry long-term responsibility for people, leaders, regions, or assignments. Their intercession is not dramatic—it is faithful. They stand when others rotate out. They cover quietly while others respond urgently.

Gap-standers are essential for sustainability. Scripture describes this role as "standing in the gap" when others cannot or will not.[4] This role requires endurance more than intensity.

When gap-standers are pressured to function like emergency responders, they burn out. Their authority lies in consistency, not escalation.

Warfare Intercessors: Those Who Confront Directly

Some intercessors are specifically graced for confrontation. They engage resistance directly. They dismantle strongholds, cancel assignments, and exercise authority decisively. Their prayers often involve command rather than petition.

Warfare intercessors must be deeply grounded in identity and Scripture, because this role carries weight. Jesus delegated authority to confront the enemy, but that authority was always exercised under alignment, not impulse.[5]

When warfare intercessors operate outside assignment or without confirmation, damage can occur. This role requires maturity, not bravado.

Stabilizers: Those Who Maintain Order

Not every intercessor is assigned to engage crisis directly. Some are stabilizers. They maintain peace, clarity, and spiritual order during or after intense moments. They help environments recalibrate. They ensure prayer does not descend into chaos.

Paul reminds the church that God is not the author of confusion, even in spiritual expression.[6] Stabilizers help ensure that discernment is preserved and authority is not diluted by disorder.

This role is often overlooked but absolutely necessary.

Why Confusion of Roles Weakens Intercession

When intercessors do not understand their role, several things occur simultaneously. Some overextend. Others withdraw. Some compete. Others feel unnecessary. The situation room becomes noisy rather than strategic.

Dutch Sheets emphasizes that effective corporate intercession requires agreement, alignment, and clearly defined focus.[7] Without role clarity, prayer becomes overlapping sound rather than unified enforcement.

God does not reward noise. He responds to alignment.

Roles Are Assigned, Not Chosen

One of the most important truths this chapter establishes is that roles in intercession are assigned by God, not selected by desire. Some intercessors gravitate toward high-intensity roles because they appear more powerful or visible. Others avoid responsibility because of fear.

Neither approach honors God.

Scripture teaches that gifts and functions are distributed according to God's wisdom, not human preference.[8] Trusting God's assignment produces peace. Resisting it produces frustration.

Roles May Shift by Season

Roles are not always permanent. God may shift function based on season, maturity, or assignment. A watcher may become a gap-stander. A warfare intercessor may be called into stabilization. What must remain constant is submission to God's direction.

Clinging to an expired role creates imbalance.

Why Comparison Is Dangerous in the Situation Room

Comparison introduces insecurity and pride simultaneously. One intercessor feels inferior. Another feels superior. Both outcomes weaken authority.

Paul warns that comparison within the body leads to disorder rather than edification.[9] Intercession thrives when intercessors honor difference without competition.

Functioning in Your Role Produces Confidence

When intercessors understand and accept their role, prayer becomes lighter—not because responsibility is reduced, but because alignment removes strain. Confidence increases. Authority sharpens. Endurance strengthens.

Intercessors stop striving to sound spiritual and start functioning spiritually.

The Situation Room Requires Trust

Every role in the situation room depends on trust—trust in God, trust in leadership, and trust in one another. Watchers must trust that alerts will be honored. Gap-standers must trust that coverage matters. Warfare intercessors must trust timing. Stabilizers must trust restraint.

Trust allows coordination.

A Call to Role Discernment

This chapter invites intercessors to stop asking, "What do I want to do?" and begin asking, "How has God positioned me to serve?"

Intercession is not about preference—it is about placement.

When roles are honored, the situation room functions with clarity, authority, and peace.

Footnotes

1. 1 Corinthians 12:18 (KJV).
2. Nehemiah 4:16–18 (KJV).
3. Isaiah 62:6 (KJV).
4. Ezekiel 22:30 (KJV).
5. Luke 10:19 (KJV).
6. 1 Corinthians 14:33 (KJV).
7. Dutch Sheets, Intercessory Prayer (Ventura, CA: Regal Books, 1996), 188–194.
8. Romans 12:6 (KJV).
9. 2 Corinthians 10:12 (KJV).

CHAPTER 10
QUESTIONS EVERY INTERCESSOR MUST ANSWER

Intercession cannot be sustained on passion alone. At some point, every intercessor must pause—not to pray louder, but to look inward. Scripture consistently teaches that spiritual authority is inseparable from spiritual alignment. Before God entrusts greater clarity, He often requires honest examination.

This chapter is not about condemnation. It is about calibration.

Throughout Scripture, those who carried responsibility before God were required to ask themselves difficult questions. Not questions of gifting, but of posture. Not questions of ability, but of alignment. Intercession that is never examined eventually drifts. Intercession that is regularly examined becomes sharp, disciplined, and trustworthy.

The Necessity of Self-Examination in Intercession

Intercessors are often so focused on covering others that they neglect to examine themselves. Yet Scripture makes it clear that effective spiritual leadership—including intercessory leadership—requires ongoing self-assessment before God.

David, one of Scripture's most effective intercessors and leaders, understood this necessity when he prayed, "Search me, O God, and know my heart… and see if there be any wicked way in me."[1] This was not insecurity—it was wisdom. David understood that blind spots compromise authority.

Intercessors who refuse examination eventually pray from habit rather than discernment.

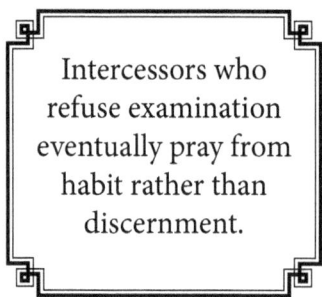

Intercessors who refuse examination eventually pray from habit rather than discernment.

Am I Praying From Assignment or Emotion?

One of the most critical questions every intercessor must answer is whether their prayer is rooted in assignment or emotion. Emotion may alert the intercessor that something is happening, but it is never meant to define the response.

Emotion-driven intercession often feels urgent but lacks clarity. It produces intensity without resolution. Over time, this creates exhaustion rather than fruit.

Assignment-driven intercession, by contrast, carries peace even in urgency. It produces focus, restraint, and authority. God never burdens an intercessor without intending to provide instruction. When prayer feels heavy but unclear, the issue is often not resistance—it is lack of discernment.

Paul's instruction to pray "with understanding" was not optional.[2] Understanding governs authority.

Do I Know What Season I Am In?

Intercession is seasonal. God does not ask the same thing of an intercessor in every phase of life. Some seasons require vigilance. Others require confrontation. Others require rest, renewal, or transition.

Intercessors who fail to recognize season often attempt to operate in expired authority. What once flowed easily begins to feel forced. Clarity diminishes. Fatigue increases.

Scripture reminds us that there is "a time for every purpose under heaven."[3] Discernment includes recognizing when God is shifting the nature of an assignment.

This question is not about effectiveness—it is about obedience.

Am I Hearing God, or Filling the Silence?

Silence exposes the condition of the intercessor's soul. Many people speak quickly in prayer because silence feels uncomfortable. But silence is often where God clarifies instruction.

Intercessors must ask whether their prayer life allows space for God to speak—or whether prayer has become a monologue rather than a dialogue.

Jesus modeled prayer that involved withdrawal, listening, and submission, not constant speech.[4] Intercessors who never pause to listen eventually pray their own thoughts rather than heaven's will.

Accuracy requires hearing.

Is This Burden Mine to Carry?

Not every burden felt by an intercessor is meant to be carried long-term. Some burdens are alerts. Others are invitations to pray briefly and release. Some are warnings. Others are assignments.

> Intercessors must learn to release what God has not given them to steward.

One of the most damaging assumptions in intercession is the belief that feeling something means responsibility for it. God never intended intercessors to carry what He did not assign.

Jesus Himself did not heal every sick person in Israel. He healed according to the Father's direction.[5] Limitation was not failure—it was obedience.

Intercessors must learn to release what God has not given them to steward.

79

Am I Interceding or Performing?

This question is uncomfortable, but necessary. Prayer can subtly shift from obedience into performance—especially in corporate settings. When prayer becomes performative, discernment fades and authority weakens.

Jesus warned against prayer designed to be seen rather than aligned.[6] True intercession is often unseen, uncelebrated, and unacknowledged—but it is effective.

Intercessors must ask whether they are praying to be heard by heaven or by people.

Do I Have Scriptural Alignment for What I Am Praying?

Scripture anchors intercession. When prayer drifts away from the Word, it becomes vulnerable to emotion, assumption, and error. God honors prayer that aligns with His revealed will.

The Word does not restrict intercession—it sharpens it.

Intercessors should be able to connect their prayer to Scripture, not as a formality, but as confirmation of alignment. Scripture ensures that prayer is governed by truth rather than imagination.

As E. M. Bounds observed, prayer that lacks grounding in Scripture often lacks staying power.[7]

Correction is a gift, not a threat. Intercessors who resist correction often stagnate spiritually. God refines those He trusts.

Am I Guarding What God Reveals?

God often reveals sensitive information to intercessors. How that information is handled determines whether trust increases or decreases. Revelation is not an invitation to speak—it is a responsibility to pray.

Intercessors must examine whether they have been faithful with what God has already revealed. Gossip, premature sharing, or fear-based interpretation compromises authority.

God entrusts more to those who guard what they are given.

Am I Willing to Be Corrected?

Correction is a gift, not a threat. Intercessors who resist correction often stagnate spiritually. God refines those He trusts.

Apollos was powerful, gifted, and sincere—but still needed correction to become more accurate.[8] Intercessors must remain teachable, humble, and responsive.

Accuracy matters more than reputation.

Am I Sustaining This Assignment With God's Strength or My Own?

This question determines longevity. Intercession sustained by human effort eventually collapses. Intercession sustained by God's strength endures.

Isaiah reminds us that those who wait upon the Lord renew strength—they do not deplete it.[9] When prayer consistently drains rather than strengthens, something is misaligned.

God does not call intercessors to exhaustion—He calls them to endurance.

The Gift of Honest Questions

These questions are not meant to discourage. They are meant to refine. Intercessors who ask hard questions before God remain clear, grounded, and effective.

Self-examination is not weakness. It is wisdom.

When intercessors refuse examination, prayer becomes routine. When they embrace it, prayer becomes precise.

Prayer

Father, search my heart and align my spirit. Remove anything in me that distorts discernment or weakens authority. Teach me to pray from obedience, not emotion; from listening, not assumption; from assignment, not pressure. I submit my intercession to Your refining hand.

Footnotes

1. Psalm 139:23–24 (KJV).
2. 1 Corinthians 14:15 (KJV).
3. Ecclesiastes 3:1 (KJV).
4. Mark 1:35 (KJV).
5. John 5:19 (KJV).
6. Matthew 6:5–6 (KJV).
7. E. M. Bounds, Power Through Prayer (Grand Rapids: Baker Books, 1991), 101–108.
8. Acts 18:24–26 (KJV).
9. Isaiah 40:31 (KJV).

CHAPTER 11
A PRAYER FOR THE INTERCESSOR

Intercessors spend their lives covering others. They watch while others rest. They carry while others are unaware. They stand when others retreat. Yet one of the most overlooked truths in intercessory ministry is this: intercessors also need prayer.

Scripture never presents intercessors as self-sustaining. Strength, clarity, endurance, and discernment are not produced internally—they are received. When intercessors attempt to survive on discipline alone, fatigue eventually replaces focus. When they rely solely on emotional zeal, burnout follows. But when intercessors remain rooted in God's renewing grace, they endure with clarity and peace.

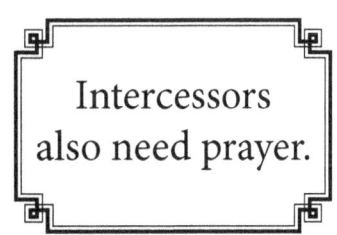

Intercessors also need prayer.

This chapter is not instruction. It is covering.

The Hidden Cost of Intercession

Intercession extracts a cost that is rarely visible. Because much of an intercessor's work happens in silence and secrecy, the toll often goes unnoticed—even by the intercessor themselves. Over time, fatigue may surface as irritability, discouragement, numbness, or withdrawal. None of these are signs of failure. They are signals that renewal is required.

Scripture acknowledges this reality when it exhorts believers not to grow weary in well-doing.[1] Weariness is not sin—but ignoring it can be dangerous.

God never rebukes intercessors for needing renewal. He invites them into it.

Strength Comes From Waiting, Not Striving

One of the great misconceptions in prayer culture is that strength is produced by doing more. Scripture teaches the opposite. Strength is renewed by waiting.

"But they that wait upon the LORD shall renew their strength…" (Isaiah 40:31, KJV)

Waiting is not inactivity—it is dependence. Intercessors who refuse to pause eventually attempt to carry spiritual weight without divine supply. When prayer becomes draining instead of sustaining, the issue is rarely the assignment; it is the absence of renewal.

God designed intercession to be fueled by His presence, not human endurance.

The Need for Ongoing Covering

Paul regularly asked others to pray for him, despite his spiritual authority and maturity.[2] This reveals an essential truth: no one outgrows the need for prayer. Intercessors, in particular, must be covered because they are consistently exposed to spiritual tension.

Intercessors who neglect their own covering often become vulnerable to discouragement, isolation, or spiritual fatigue. Covering is not weakness—it is wisdom.

God's Commitment to the Intercessor

Scripture assures intercessors that God Himself is committed to their protection.

"But the Lord is faithful, who shall stablish you, and keep you from evil." (2 Thessalonians 3:3, KJV)

God does not merely assign intercessors—He guards them. He stabilizes them. He strengthens them. But this strength must be received, not assumed.

Intercessors who attempt to be strong without God's supply often become hardened instead of strengthened.

Emotional Recovery Is Part of Spiritual Health

Intercessors feel deeply. This sensitivity is not a flaw—it is part of the calling. But emotion must be processed, not suppressed. When intercessors ignore emotional strain, it often resurfaces as exhaustion or detachment.

David understood this when he poured out his soul before God repeatedly.[3] Emotional honesty before God is not weakness—it is alignment.

God restores emotional equilibrium so discernment remains clear.

The Grace to Continue

Intercession is rarely rewarded immediately. Often, the intercessor never sees the fruit of what they prayed. This requires grace to continue without affirmation.

Hebrews reminds us that faithfulness often precedes visible outcome.[4] God honors endurance even when results are delayed.

Intercessors must be strengthened not by results, but by trust.

Rest Is Not Retreat

One of the most spiritual acts an intercessor can practice is rest. Rest is not disengagement from assignment—it is obedience to God's design. Jesus Himself withdrew regularly, not because He lacked power, but because He honored divine rhythm.[5]

Intercessors who refuse rest eventually confuse exhaustion with devotion. God restores through rest.

The Prayer That Covers the Intercessor

This chapter culminates in prayer—not as a conclusion, but as an infusion. This prayer is meant to be read slowly, prayed personally, and revisited often.

A Prayer for the Intercessor

Father,

I come before You acknowledging that You are the source of my strength, not my discipline, not my endurance, and not my emotion. I thank You for trusting me with intercession, for inviting me into moments of discernment, and for assigning me to stand where others cannot.

I ask now for renewal. Where weariness has crept in unnoticed, restore me. Where emotional weight has accumulated, lighten me. Where discouragement has whispered quietly, silence it with truth.

Strengthen my inner man according to Your Word. Guard my heart from bitterness, my mind from confusion, and my spirit from fatigue. Teach me to wait upon You without guilt and to rest without fear.

Protect me from burnout disguised as faithfulness. Protect me from isolation disguised as maturity. Protect me from striving disguised as obedience. Renew my sensitivity without overwhelming me. Sharpen my discernment without exhausting me. Sustain my assignment without draining my soul.

I receive Your grace to continue. I receive Your peace to remain steady. I receive Your strength for the long watch.

In Jesus' name. Amen.

Closing Exhortation

Intercessors are not machines. They are servants. God does not demand endless output—He promises faithful supply.

Those who are renewed pray with clarity.

Those who are covered pray with confidence.

Those who are strengthened endure.

Footnotes

1. Galatians 6:9 (KJV).
2. Ephesians 6:18–20 (KJV).
3. Psalm 62:8 (KJV).
4. Hebrews 10:36 (KJV).
5. Mark 6:31 (KJV).

CHAPTER 12
FINAL CHARGE—WE WILL ALWAYS BE IN THE SITUATION ROOM

Intercession does not end when the prayer gathering closes. It does not pause when worship fades or when the moment feels calm. For the trained intercessor, there is no such thing as being "off assignment." There are only shifts in posture, awareness, and response.

This is the final truth every intercessor must embrace:

We are always in the situation room.

Not because we are anxious, but because we are entrusted. Not because danger is constant, but because vigilance is required. Intercession is not an event—it is a way of seeing, listening, and responding in partnership with heaven.

This final charge is not meant to inspire fear. It is meant to anchor responsibility.

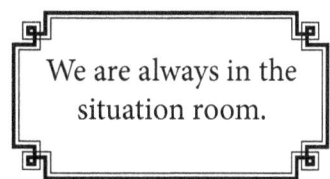

We are always in the situation room.

Watchfulness as a Way of Life

Scripture consistently portrays watchfulness as a spiritual discipline, not a temporary state. Jesus repeatedly instructed His disciples to "watch," not merely in moments of crisis, but as a posture of readiness.[1] Watchfulness does not mean suspicion. It means attentiveness.

Intercessors are trained to notice what others overlook. They sense shifts before language forms. They recognize when peace is genuine and when it is artificial. This awareness does not turn off—it matures.

The situation room is not a place intercessors enter occasionally; it is the lens through which they view life.

Authority Requires Stewardship

Authority is not self-generated. It is stewarded. Scripture teaches that authority is always connected to responsibility. "Unto whomsoever much is given, of him shall be much required."[2] Intercessors are given insight not as a privilege, but as a trust.

God does not reveal so intercessors can feel important. He reveals so they can respond accurately.

When intercessors misuse authority—by speaking prematurely, reacting emotionally, or abandoning discernment—authority weakens. But when authority is stewarded with humility and restraint, it increases.

The Temptation to Relax Spiritually

One of the greatest dangers for trained intercessors is spiritual complacency. After seasons of intensity, there is often a temptation to relax vigilance, assuming the assignment has ended. But Scripture never presents vigilance as seasonal.

Peter warns believers to remain sober and vigilant because resistance often appears when attention drifts.[3] The enemy rarely announces attacks loudly. He waits for gaps.

Intercessors do not live in fear—but they do not live unaware.

Prayer That Moves Heaven Quietly

One of the marks of mature intercession is quiet effectiveness. Early in spiritual development, intercessors often equate power with volume and movement. Over time, maturity produces restraint.

James writes that "the effectual fervent prayer of a righteous man availeth much."[4] Fervency here does not describe noise—it describes alignment, persistence, and righteousness. Many of the most powerful prayers are spoken quietly, clearly, and without spectacle.

The situation room is not loud. It is focused.

Guarding the Assignment Beyond the Gathering

Intercession does not remain confined to prayer meetings. It follows intercessors into daily life. Conversations are filtered. Information is weighed. Urgency is discerned. Words are guarded.

Jesus taught that faithfulness is proven in what is unseen.[5] Intercessors must guard their mouths, their reactions, and their interpretations. Not every impression is meant to be shared. Not every insight is meant to be spoken.

Some victories are won because intercessors remained silent and prayed.

Living Alert Without Living Anxious

This chapter does not call intercessors into hyper-vigilance or spiritual paranoia. It calls them into disciplined awareness. There is a difference.

Anxious people scan for danger.

Trained intercessors listen for instruction.

Peace does not mean disengagement. Peace means confidence that God is ruling while we remain attentive to His direction.

Accountability Comes With Insight

The more God reveals, the greater the accountability. This is not punitive—it is protective. God corrects those He trusts because accuracy matters.

Intercessors who understand this welcome refinement. They do not resist correction. They understand that precision protects people.

Hebrews reminds us that discipline is evidence of sonship, not rejection.[6]

We Are Positioned for the Long Watch

This book has not trained you for moments—it has trained you for longevity. Intercession is not sustained by adrenaline. It is sustained by obedience, rhythm, and renewal.

Some seasons will feel quiet. Others will feel urgent. Some moments will require silence. Others will require command. The intercessor who endures is the one who knows how to shift without losing posture.

The long watch requires maturity.

A Final Responsibility

From this point forward, ignorance is no longer an excuse. You have been given language for discernment, structure for response, and clarity for assignment. With that comes responsibility.

You now understand:

- How to shift postures
- How to recognize threat levels
- How to guard revelation
- How to respond without panic
- How to stand without performing

God trusts intercessors who understand weight.

Final Charge

This is your charge:

Remain alert, but remain anchored.

Remain discerning, but remain humble.

Remain faithful, even when unseen.

You are not called to pray loudly—you are called to pray accurately.

You are not called to react—you are called to respond.

You are not called to feel deeply—you are called to discern clearly.

You are entrusted.

And because you are entrusted, you will always be in the situation room.

Prayer of Commission

Father,

I receive the responsibility that comes with discernment. I choose vigilance without fear, obedience without striving, and endurance without pride. Guard my heart, sharpen my hearing, and steady my spirit. Teach me to remain alert in peace and faithful in pressure.

I commit to steward what You reveal, to guard what You entrust, and to respond according to Your will. I accept this charge—not as burden, but as honor.

In Jesus' name. Amen.

Footnotes

1. Matthew 26:41 (KJV).
2. Luke 12:48 (KJV).
3. 1 Peter 5:8 (KJV).
4. James 5:16 (KJV).
5. Luke 16:10 (KJV).
6. Hebrews 12:6–11 (KJV).

CONCLUSION
TRAINED, TRUSTED, AND POSITIONED

Intercession does not end with understanding. It begins there.

This book was never meant to create more informed intercessors—it was written to form trusted ones. Knowledge alone does not move heaven. Alignment does. Obedience does. Discernment does. What you now carry is not simply language for prayer, but responsibility for posture.

Intercession is not something you add to your spiritual life. It becomes the way you listen, the way you respond, and the way you stand.

By this point, one truth should be unmistakably clear: God does not entrust weight to the untrained. He entrusts it to those who have learned restraint, discernment, and faithfulness over time. Intercession is not dramatic—it is disciplined. It is not loud—it is precise. It is not reactive—it is responsive.

From Emotion to Stewardship

Many intercessors begin their journey through emotion. They feel deeply, respond quickly, and carry heavily. God does not despise that sensitivity—it is often the doorway into calling. But He never intends emotion to remain the governing force.

This book has traced the journey from emotional awareness to spiritual stewardship.

Stewardship asks different questions than emotion.

Emotion asks, "What do I feel?"

Stewardship asks, "What has God assigned?"

Emotion asks, "How urgent does this feel?"

Stewardship asks, "What response does heaven require?"

The maturation of an intercessor is marked by this shift. God trusts those who can feel without reacting, perceive without panicking, and stand without performing.

The Weight You Now Carry

If you have read this book carefully, you are no longer praying blindly. You now understand gates, posture, timing, authority, assignment, and discernment. That understanding carries weight.

Scripture teaches that increased revelation brings increased accountability.[1] This is not meant to intimidate—it is meant to anchor responsibility. God never reveals in order to burden; He reveals in order to partner.

You are not accountable for what you did not know.

But you are accountable for what you now understand.

This is not a threat. It is an honor.

The Quiet Nature of Trusted Intercession

One of the most difficult adjustments for many intercessors is accepting how quiet trusted intercession often becomes. There is less explaining, less announcing, less processing aloud. As discernment sharpens, restraint increases.

God does not need intercessors who narrate the battle.

He needs intercessors who win it quietly.

Jesus Himself modeled this restraint. He withdrew often. He spoke selectively. He responded only to what the Father showed Him.[2] The greatest authority He exercised was often unseen by crowds.

Intercession matures into silence not because it has less power—but because it has more.

The Longevity God Is After

God is not training intercessors for moments—He is training them for decades. Emotional intensity can sustain short bursts of prayer. Only discernment and obedience can sustain a lifetime of watchfulness.

Scripture repeatedly emphasizes endurance, not excitement.[3] Endurance requires rhythm, rest, humility, and renewal. It requires knowing when to stand and when to sit. When to speak and when to wait. When to war and when to worship.

Longevity is the fruit of obedience repeated quietly over time.

Generational Responsibility

Intercession is never meant to end with one generation. What God trains in one season is meant to be stewarded, modeled, and passed on. Intercessors who mature must eventually become trainers, whether formally or informally.

Not all teaching happens from platforms. Much of it happens through posture, restraint, and example.

You are now responsible not only for how you pray—but for what others learn about prayer by watching you.

Paul understood this when he instructed believers to imitate his way of life, not just his words.[4] Intercession that is modeled accurately reproduces maturity.

Guarding Against Two Final Dangers

As this book closes, two dangers must be named clearly.

The first is spiritual pride. Discernment does not make an intercessor superior—it makes them accountable. Authority that is not clothed in humility eventually collapses.

The second is spiritual fatigue disguised as faithfulness. God never asked intercessors to destroy themselves for the assignment. He asked them to obey Him within it. Rest is not retreat—it is alignment.

Jesus invited His disciples to rest even while the work remained unfinished.[5] That invitation still stands.

A Settled Identity

You are not called to be dramatic. You are not called to be visible.

You are not called to be constantly intense. You are called to be faithful.

Faithfulness is quiet. It is repetitive. It is unseen. And it is deeply honored by heaven.

God does not measure intercessors by volume, tears, or longevity of prayer sessions. He measures them by obedience, accuracy, and trustworthiness.

Final Exhortation

From this point forward, let your intercession be marked by clarity rather than chaos, restraint rather than reaction, and obedience rather than emotion.

Stand when God says stand.

Speak when God says speak.

Remain silent when God says wait.

Trust that heaven sees what earth never will.

You have been trained.

You have been trusted.

You have been positioned.

Remain faithful.

Closing Prayer

Father,

I thank You for the training You have given and the clarity You have released. I receive the responsibility that comes with understanding. Guard my heart from pride and my spirit from fatigue. Teach me to remain faithful in silence and obedient in pressure.

Let my intercession be accurate, disciplined, and enduring. May what You have formed in me now protect others quietly and effectively.

I commit to this calling—not as a burden, but as a trust.

In Jesus' name. Amen.

Footnotes

1. Luke 12:48 (KJV).
2. John 5:19 (KJV).
3. Hebrews 12:1 (KJV).
4. 1 Corinthians 11:1 (KJV).
5. Mark 6:31 (KJV).

GLOSSARY OF TERMS

Assignment

A specific responsibility given by God to an intercessor for prayer coverage, vigilance, or action. Assignment defines scope, focus, and authority. Praying outside of assignment often leads to exhaustion and diminished effectiveness, while praying within assignment produces clarity and endurance.

Authority

The spiritual right and delegated power given by God to enforce His will on earth. Authority in intercession flows from alignment with God's Word, obedience to His instruction, and confidence in covenant—not from volume, emotion, or longevity of prayer.

Burden

A spiritual awareness or weight placed upon an intercessor to alert them that something requires attention. A burden is not always an assignment. Some burdens signal the need for brief prayer and release, while others indicate sustained responsibility. Discernment is required to distinguish between the two.

Discernment

The Spirit-enabled ability to perceive what is happening beyond natural sight, including timing, intent, spiritual formation, and threat level. Discernment governs intercession, ensuring that prayer responds accurately rather than emotionally.

Emotional Intercession

Prayer that is driven primarily by feeling rather than revelation. While emotion may accompany intercession, it must never govern it. Emotional intercession often produces release for the intercessor but limited strategic impact.

Endurance

The grace to remain faithful in intercession over time, even when results are delayed or unseen. Endurance is sustained by obedience and renewal, not by intensity or adrenaline.

Gate

A point of access in the spiritual realm where influence, authority, or movement is permitted. Gates may involve minds, relationships, leadership, institutions, or territories. Intercessors are trained to recognize, guard, and close gates through prayer.

Gap-Stander

An intercessor assigned to provide consistent, long-term prayer coverage for a person, group, leader, or region. Gap-standers are marked by faithfulness rather than intensity and often labor quietly over extended seasons.

Holy of Holies

A spiritual posture of deep reverence, stillness, and proximity to God where instruction, strategy, and authority are received. In intercession, entering the Holy of Holies refers to praying from a place of listening and submission rather than expression or performance.

Intercession

The act of standing between heaven and earth on behalf of others to enforce God's will, intercept threats, and protect purpose. Intercession is not merely asking God to act—it is partnering with Him through discernment, obedience, and authority.

Intercessor

A believer entrusted by God to pray strategically, discern accurately, and stand faithfully on behalf of others. An intercessor is not defined by prayer volume or emotion, but by obedience, discipline, and stewardship.

Monitoring

A posture of alertness and attentiveness in prayer when no immediate threat is present. Monitoring involves watching, listening, and gathering spiritual intelligence without unnecessary escalation.

Posture

The internal spiritual position from which an intercessor prays. Posture may include worship, listening, command, standing, or silence, depending on what the moment requires. Correct posture precedes effective response.

Revelation

Insight or information given by God to an intercessor regarding what is forming, threatened, or required. Revelation is given for prayer, not discussion, and must be stewarded with confidentiality and humility.

Silence

A disciplined spiritual practice in which the intercessor refrains from speaking in order to hear God clearly. Silence is not inactivity; it is preparation for accurate response.

Situation Room

A metaphor used in this book to describe the disciplined spiritual environment where intercessors receive intelligence, assess threat levels, and respond strategically. The situation room is governed by restraint, confidentiality, and obedience.

Stabilizer

An intercessor assigned to maintain peace, clarity, and order during or after intense spiritual moments. Stabilizers help prevent chaos and ensure that authority is not diluted by disorder.

Stewardship

The responsible handling of spiritual authority, revelation, assignment, and endurance. Stewardship emphasizes faithfulness over visibility and obedience over impulse.

Threat Level

The degree of spiritual urgency present in a situation, determining the appropriate posture and response in intercession. Misreading threat levels often leads to overreaction or delayed intervention.

Vigilance

A sustained posture of alertness and attentiveness in prayer. Vigilance is not fear-based awareness, but disciplined readiness rooted in trust and discernment.

Warfare Intercessor

An intercessor specifically graced to confront resistance, dismantle strongholds, and enforce authority directly. This role requires maturity, restraint, and strong grounding in Scripture and identity.

Watcher / Watchman

An intercessor assigned to discern spiritual shifts, detect early warning signs, and alert others through prayer. Watchers often perceive danger before it manifests and play a critical role in prevention.

Closing Note on Language

The terms in this glossary are not meant to create hierarchy or exclusivity. They exist to provide clarity, shared understanding, and precision for those committed to disciplined intercession. Language sharpens discernment, and discernment preserves authority.

BIBLIOGRAPHY

Scripture

The Holy Bible, King James Version. Peabody, MA: Hendrickson Publishers, 2012.

Books

Bounds, Edward M. *Power Through Prayer.* Grand Rapids: Baker Books, 1991.

Fee, Gordon D. *God's Empowering Presence: The Holy Spirit in the Letters of Paul.* Peabody, MA: Hendrickson Publishers, 1994.

Murray, Andrew. *With Christ in the School of Prayer.* New Kensington, PA: Whitaker House, 1981.

Nee, Watchman. *The Authority of the Believer.* New York: Christian Fellowship Publishers, 1972.

Prince, Derek. *Shaping History Through Prayer and Fasting.* Old Tappan, NJ: Chosen Books, 1997.

Sheets, Dutch. *Intercessory Prayer: How God Can Use Your Prayers to Move Heaven and Earth.* Ventura, CA: Regal Books, 1996.

Biblical Commentaries & Reference Works

Brown, Francis, S. R. Driver, and Charles A. Briggs. *The Brown-Driver-Briggs Hebrew and English Lexicon.* Peabody, MA: Hendrickson Publishers, 2003.

Strong, James. *The Exhaustive Concordance of the Bible.* Peabody, MA: Hendrickson Publishers, 1996.

Vine, W. E. *Vine's Complete Expository Dictionary of Old and New Testament Words.* Nashville: Thomas Nelson, 1996.

Theology, Spiritual Formation, and Prayer

Bonhoeffer, Dietrich. *Life Together.* New York: Harper & Row, 1954.

Foster, Richard J. *Prayer: Finding the Heart's True Home.* San Francisco: HarperOne, 1992.

Tozer, A. W. *The Pursuit of God.* Harrisburg, PA: Christian Publications, 1948.

Church Leadership & Spiritual Discipline

Willard, Dallas. *The Spirit of the Disciplines.* New York: HarperOne, 1988.

Yong, Amos. *The Spirit Poured Out on All Flesh: Pentecostalism and the Possibility of Global Theology.* Grand Rapids: Baker Academic, 2005.

Historical & Biblical Studies (Supporting Context)

Keener, Craig S. *The IVP Bible Background Commentary: New Testament.* Downers Grove, IL: InterVarsity Press, 1993.

Wright, N. T. *After You Believe: Why Christian Character Matters.* New York: HarperOne, 2010.

ABOUT THE AUTHOR

Barbara Palmer is a pastor, award-winning nonprofit executive, author, speaker, and mentor with more than thirty years of distinguished leadership in ministry, community development, and family advocacy. She is the Founder and CEO of Kingdom Kare, Inc., a multifaceted nonprofit organization serving children, families, and underserved communities through early childhood education, youth mentorship, teen parent support, violence-prevention initiatives, and holistic family services.

Barbara is the recipient of numerous leadership and community impact awards recognizing her excellence in nonprofit innovation, faith-based leadership, and transformational service. She is also the author of five books and has collaborated on projects with entertainment and business leader Master P, further expanding her influence at the intersection of culture, faith, and community empowerment.

Widely respected for her prophetic insight and compassionate yet strategic leadership, Barbara is sought after nationally to help grassroots and emerging organizations build capacity, strengthen infrastructure, and position themselves for sustainable growth. She is particularly known for her ability to bridge the gap between faith-based organizations and government systems—guiding churches and nonprofits to operate with both spiritual integrity and regulatory excellence.

Barbara writes from lived experience. As a mother who has survived the loss of a child and a woman who has endured seasons of deep personal betrayal, her voice carries uncommon authenticity and authority. She speaks candidly about grief, healing, leadership, boundaries, and restoration, offering wisdom that resonates with women navigating loss, transition, and calling. Her message is one of hope grounded in truth and strength forged through surrender.

In addition to her nonprofit leadership, Barbara is a sought-after speaker and mentor, equipping women leaders, pastors' wives, entrepreneurs, and ministry builders to lead with clarity, courage, and wholeness. She is deeply passionate about helping women discover their voice, steward their influence, and walk boldly in both faith and leadership.

Barbara resides with her husband, Apostle Antonio Palmer. Together, they continue to lead, teach, and mentor individuals and organizations across the country—leaving a legacy rooted in faith, service, and transformational impact.

For bookings, speaking, workshops, or conferences, Dr. Barbara Palmer can be reached at the following:

Email

info@IAmBarbaraPalmer.com

Social Media

Facebook | Instagram | Threads | TikTok

@IAmBarbaraPalmer

Website

www.IAmBarbaraPalmer.com

www.ingramcontent.com/pod-product-compliance
Lightning Source LLC
Chambersburg PA
CBHW051215120626
46547CB00013B/1367